Reaching for a Star

*A Memoir of My Life, My Music, and My Friendship
with Famed Singer Frankie Laine*

CRAIG CRONBAUGH

authorHOUSE™

1663 LIBERTY DRIVE, SUITE 200
BLOOMINGTON, INDIANA 47403
(800) 839-8640
WWW.AUTHORHOUSE.COM

First published by AuthorHouse 12/27/05

ISBN: 1-4208-0391-3 (sc)
ISBN: 1-4208-0390-5 (dj)

Library of Congress Control Number: 2004098045

Printed in the United States of America
Bloomington, Indiana

This book is printed on acid-free paper.

Front photographs:
Left: Craig Cronbaugh and Frankie Laine at Frankie's home—San Diego July 17, 2000
Right: Frankie Laine—a new star (circa 1950)

Cover and jacket design: Craig Cronbaugh
Front and back color photographs: Marlene Cronbaugh
The photographs on the inside pages are from the author's private collection.

To Marlene, my beautiful wife . . .

Thanks for loving me and believing in me.

Special Thanks To:

Frankie Laine, for your friendship

Mary-Jo Coombs, Tony Cooper, and Jimmy Marino, for your assistance

Jim and Rosemarie Skaine, for believing in my book project

Latisha Purk, for being my beautiful daughter

Payton Kaye Brown and Keon Michael Purk, for being my inspiration

Copyeditor:

Sue Fetters

In Memory Of:

My friends:

Danny Aarhus, Rick Boddicker, and Helen Snow

My beloved mom, Helen Cronbaugh

and

My brother, Scott Cronbaugh

The following celebrity quotes were individually presented by each star to Craig Cronbaugh exclusively for:

Reaching for a Star

"I've always enjoyed very much listening to Frankie Laine sing. His good, strong voice could sing any type of song, whether it was a gentle, heartfelt ballad, a soulful blues number, or an up-tempo, rousing one. No matter what he sang, it was always with gusto—a great voice, one that has endured over the years."
—TERESA BREWER, popular singer and recording artist

"Frankie *is* 'Mr. Rhythm.' It was a joy singing with him."
—CONNIE HAINES, big band and popular singer, recording artist, featured on *The Frankie Laine Show* on television

"Frankie Laine is an original. When you hear a Frankie Laine recording, it can only be him. No one else has that sound! I had the pleasure of performing with him at the San Remo Song Festival in Italy and watched the master at work. He brought the audience to their feet with his Italian song the Laine way! Very few careers will encompass the breadth of Frankie Laine! Bravo!!"
—GENE PITNEY, popular singer, recording artist, and songwriter

"It was always a pleasure to work with Frankie. Besides being a very nice gentleman, he was always well prepared and ready to go to work."
—JO STAFFORD, big band and popular singer, recording artist, recorded several duets with Frankie Laine

CONTENTS

PROLOGUE: *Frankie Laine* .... *xv*

    Fame .... *xv*

    Fans .... *xix*

INTRODUCTION: *Heroes* .... *xxv*

AUTHOR'S NOTE .... *xxvii*

CHAPTER ONE: *San Diego* *1*

    First Time Together—Part I *1*

    The Journey *1*

    First Time Together—Part II *4*

CHAPTER TWO: *Beginnings* *9*

CHAPTER THREE: *A Quest Realized* *63*

    First Time Together—Part III *63*

CHAPTER FOUR: *We'll Be Together Again* *91*

CHAPTER FIVE: *My Friend Helen* *111*

CHAPTER SIX: *A New Direction* *139*

CHAPTER SEVEN: *Birthday Bash* *153*

CHAPTER EIGHT: *Frankie's People* *159*

CHAPTER NINE: *Projects* *187*

CHAPTER TEN: *Up Among the Stars* *217*

ABOUT THE AUTHOR *257*

PROLOGUE
Frankie Laine

Fame

World famous recording star Frankie Laine achieved his first million-selling record, "That's My Desire," in 1947. (Frankie's version was inducted into the Grammy Hall of Fame in 1998.) Since that time, Frankie garnered over twenty gold records, including such unforgettable musical gems as "The Cry of the Wild Goose," "I Believe," "Jezebel," "Mule Train," "On the Sunny Side of the Street," "Shine," and "That Lucky Old Sun." Out of approximately seventy of Frankie's total charted hits in the United States, four were number one.

Shortly after Frankie's first hit recording, he became one of the most popular and sought after singers of the day. The Laine talent was in constant demand in nightclubs, on radio, in motion pictures, and on television. In addition to being supremely successful in the United States, Frankie also quickly rose to international stardom. Frankie's 1953 recording of "I Believe" topped the British music charts and stayed at number one for eighteen weeks, an unbeaten performance that even the Beatles never matched. Frankie charted thirty-two hits in England—four were number one. One of the highlights in Frankie's career happened in 1954 when Queen Elizabeth II selected him for a Royal Command Performance in England.

Throughout 1954 and 1955, Frankie hosted and sang on his own television musical variety show, *The Frankie Laine Show,* with singer Connie Haines. During the summers of 1955 and 1956, Frankie hosted and sang on the musical variety television show for CBS called *Frankie Laine Time.* Subsequently, one of stardom's highest honors was bestowed upon Frankie, not once, but twice, when his talent was celebrated with two stars on the Hollywood Walk of Fame—one for recording and the other for television.

Frankie, also a prolific songwriter, has collaborated with such famed tunesmiths as Hoagy Carmichael, Matt Dennis, Duke Ellington, Al Lerner, and Mel Tormé, to name a few. Frankie's composition of "We'll Be Together Again," written with Carl Fischer, is a musical classic, with renditions recorded by over a hundred artists throughout the years.

Befitting his songwriting talent, Frankie was awarded the Lifetime Achievement Award at the 27th Annual Songwriters Hall of Fame awards ceremony in New York City in 1996.

During his fabulous singing career, Frankie held contracts with four of the music industry's top recording companies: Mercury, Columbia, Capitol, and ABC. Additionally, Frankie's recordings can be found on many independent record labels, including his own Score Records.

Always willing to try new types and genres of music, Frankie, beginning with his recordings of "That Lucky Old Sun" and "Mule Train" in 1949, became a very popular singer of cowboy-type songs. Because of his unique ability, style, and ensuing popular recognition within this musical genre, Frankie was employed to sing the title tracks for several Western-flavored motion pictures during the 1950s. These movies included *Blowing Wild, Man Without a Star, Strange Lady in Town, Gunfight at the*

O.K. Corral, 3:10 to Yuma, and *Bullwhip.* Two decades later, Frankie was asked by Mel Brooks to sing the title track to Brooks' 1974 movie *Blazing Saddles,* which became a cult comedy classic.

Frankie was featured in seven motion picture musicals from 1949 to 1956. Also during this period, Frankie recorded duets with such popular songsters as Jimmy Boyd, Doris Day, the Four Lads, Patti Page, Johnnie Ray, and Jo Stafford.

Whenever Frankie describes a Frankie Laine record, he modestly refers to it as "our record," encompassing writers, musicians, arrangers, conductors, technicians, and anyone else involved in the creation of each round, grooved piece of Laine musical history.

The television Western series *Rawhide* made its debut in 1959. Frankie sang the title theme. The song was also released on a record. Not only did it become a million-seller, but it is also credited with launching the television show, which originally aired for many years. The series firmly established Clint Eastwood, who played the character "Rowdy Yates," as a star. Today, the *Rawhide* theme, sung by Frankie Laine, is one of the most popular and most recognized theme songs in the history of television.

Amazingly, Frankie also sang the title themes to two more television shows during the 1960s—*Gunslinger,* the 1961 CBS Television series starring Tony Young and Preston Foster, and *Rango,* the 1967 Spelling-Thomas ABC Television comedy series starring Tim Conway. Years later, Frankie sang the title theme featured during the first season of *The Misadventures of Sheriff Lobo,* the 1979-81 NBC Television series comedy starring Claude Akins.

In 1998, Frankie was awarded the Golden Boot Award for his significant contribution in film and television Westerns. In 2001, the

California Chapter of the Western Music Association honored Frankie with induction into the Western Music Hall of Fame.

In addition to the countless television musical guest appearances and interview shows Frankie guest-starred on as a singer, he displayed his acting talents performing roles on *Perry Mason* and *The Danny Thomas Show (Make Room for Daddy),* in the late 1950s, and *Rawhide, Bachelor Father,* and *Burke's Law,* in the early 1960s. His dramatic acting performances on *Perry Mason* and *Rawhide* are astounding.

More than any other singer, Frankie possesses the unique ability to sing several different music genres and yet make the songs believable. He aptly and equally inspires from jazz to cowboy laments and everything in between. Other great popular singers seemed to emulate only one style, failing to attain the accommodating voice needed to make song-style transitions believable.

As if he weren't prolific enough, Frankie combined musical genres in 1987 with the release of a compact disc of Western musical Americana, which he recorded with Eric Kunzel and the Cincinnati Pops Orchestra. This CD actually went on to achieve a good standing on Billboard's classical music chart.

Toward the end of the twentieth century, Frankie continued to receive accolades from both professional and lay organizations for his contributions to the entertainment industry and for his humanitarian works, which were many and included, among others, the Damon Runyon Cancer Fund, "Meals on Wheels," and the "Old Shoes" campaign (shoes for the homeless). In the late 1990s, Frankie reached out to a new generation by sharing the greatest joy of his life, his love for music. Frankie launched a project with the Salvation Army in his hometown of San Diego, to collect musical instruments for underprivileged children.

Reader's Digest Music released a three-CD set of popular Frankie Laine songs in 1997. Additionally, Frankie introduced a newly recorded jazz/pop CD entitled *Wheels of a Dream* in 1998, and was the first artist to record his own rendition of the title song from the Broadway musical *Ragtime.* Frankie unveiled yet another new CD of songs entitled *It Ain't Over 'Til It's Over* in 1999. This album was designed for people who have reached the age of retirement. At the beginning of the new century, Bear Family Records produced three multi-CD box sets of Frankie's entire Mercury Records and Columbia Records catalogs. Not to be outdone, Frankie's label, Score Records, is continually turning out CD song compilations including both old and contemporary recordings.

Frankie contributed much to twentieth-century music. Astonishingly, Frankie Laine's total worldwide record sales exceed two hundred million. Consequently, in 2000, the Women's International Center presented Frankie with the Living Legend Award.

A documentary on Frankie's life and career has recently been released on both VHS and DVD by J.F.M. International Productions, Incorporated. The documentary, entitled *Frankie Laine: An American Dreamer,* has received worldwide acclaim. Not surprisingly, during celebrity interviews, each star articulates how very much they admire Frankie and his artistry.

Fans

No one truly loves his many fans as much as Frankie. His following spans the world over. Many agree that Frankie is one of the kindest, most generous human beings in show business. Tirelessly, he will sign autographs, pose for pictures, and chat with anyone seeking his attention.

He realizes, because of his years of struggling to get to the top, that the audiences are directly responsible for his successful career.

Even though oftentimes forgotten since his heyday encompassing the late 1940s and all through the 1950s, and without the lingering acclaim of Como, Crosby, Presley, or Sinatra, people still admire Frankie's celebrity, and he continues to enjoy the respect of his peers, praise from the media, and the sincere love of his fans. Strangely, most people realize who Frankie Laine is as long as his name is mentioned alongside the songs "Mule Train" and "Rawhide," or the movie *Blazing Saddles*.

Frankie possesses a unique sound and style. Until Frankie came along, male vocalists merely crooned while putting a stranglehold on the upright microphone stand. But Frankie, who became known about the time television was getting started, not only belted out the rhythm songs he sang, but realized that a singer must also have a qualifying style of delivery. Because of this unique format, Frankie has influenced countless singers, among them Tony Bennett, Johnnie Ray, and even Elvis.

* * *

Frankie Laine never gave up endeavoring to make a singing career his goal. His was a long, difficult road. Frankie's saga is a true story of the Great American Dream. It's a tale of a young man who struggled to achieve *his* dream—a dream to make music and sing songs, and become successful in doing it. During the 1930s, Frankie survived his few exhausting years as a marathon dancer. Later, he managed to find occasional singing jobs that were both short-lived and short on pay.

Early on in his story, while attempting to find success in New York City, young Frankie bounded from club to club in his attempts to be allowed to sing on stage with the bands. Many times he had little or nothing to eat, but he pressed onward. He had no living quarters and sneaked into hotels to sleep on the floors. Ultimately, Frankie was found out and then thrown out of these establishments. At one point, when he was down to four cents in his pocket, Frankie's bed became a wooden park bench in Central Park. He used these four remaining pennies to buy four tiny Baby Ruth candy bars, rationing himself to one per day. He survived. He had a dream. Frankie somehow realized that achieving his dream was only a matter of time, but there were still to be many other struggles and disappointments over the years before his star began to shine.

Everyone can learn a valuable lesson from Frankie's persistence and the ability to keep plugging along, even when time after time, year after year, the odds seemed against him. Even through hardship, Frankie remained optimistic and to this day retains a personable and unassuming quality.

Frankie's tale is about struggle in the face of adversity, a battle he eventually won. Through his perseverance, he became a seasoned human being. He knows what it's like to be at life's lowest ebb. He knows the heartbreak of opportunities that didn't pan out, loves that didn't last, and the tribulations that take place in an imperfect world.

Through it all, Frankie acquired a humbleness that few other stars of his caliber can boast. Indeed, a story about Frankie Laine is free of a life filled with scandal. Instead, his saga is chock-full of survival tales while attempting to make it in an industry that can literally destroy a person. Fortunately, Frankie ultimately made it to success. Many others have tried and failed.

The dues Frankie paid in order to achieve the kind of stardom he enjoys undoubtedly molded his ability to relate to an audience. His years of struggle before fame have not only cultivated his soul, but also honed a voice that is something remarkable.

No wonder Frankie can sing with such emotion. No wonder he can relate so well to his listeners. No wonder Frankie can declare with complete sincerity the words that make up the title of a song he sang in his late eighties—"I Am a Singer."

Undeniably, Frankie Laine's life is a digest of the Great American Dream, and Frankie is the personification of this.

* * *

"I am a singer." When Frankie Laine sings those four words, nothing is closer to the truth. He *is* a singer. But there's more to the Frankie Laine legend than merely being labeled a singer. He's also a communicator. When Frankie sings, he *connects* with his listeners. He has the uncanny ability to convey the lyrics of a song with such feeling and emotion that the listener can actually sense his message. Through Frankie's unique interpretation of a song, the listener becomes privy to the exact feelings the lyricist intended.

The late writer Irving Stone once wrote about Frankie Laine:

> . . . *Frankie knows precisely what it is he wants to say through a song. He does not mouth words or belt out phrases he does not understand. What he sings, he feels; that is why he is able to make the listener feel the same emotion.*

Because of this special ability to communicate, the listener feels each song right along with Frankie. Listeners sense the loneliness when he sings the blues, feel whimsical when he sings a love ballad, and experience the excitement when he sings an upbeat musical number. Indeed, listeners can undergo a whole cluster of feelings while feasting their ears on the smorgasbord comprised of the many genres of music that Frankie Laine has recorded over the years. From jazz to cowboy songs. From pop to country. From ballads to inspirational songs.

With his fabulous singing voice, Frankie shares a part of himself with each listener. Perhaps this is why he is so special, so endearing. Consequently, it's not surprising that Frankie Laine continues to exemplify the status of music legend, not only among his fans, but among music lovers the world over.

INTRODUCTION
Heroes

Here are a few words about heroes. Everyone needs at least one hero. Heroes come in all genders, shapes, sizes, and colors. A hero doesn't have prerequisites. A hero can be pauper or king, common or majestic, family or celebrity, dead or alive. We all need them. A hero is someone who inspires us. A hero is someone who makes us feel good. A hero makes us feel glad we are living and a part of this planet. A hero may cause us to feel philosophical—to look at the world in a different way—a special way. Heroes can be thought of as the truest of admired souls. We may choose to emulate our heroes. There is nothing wrong with pretending to be like the one(s) you admire. Living vicariously as our heroes may very well help us through times of fear, anger, or sorrow.

I have many heroes. It is my hope that you, too, will supply yourself with one or more heroes. Some of my heroes are personal friends. Quite a few of my heroes are celebrities. Many of the celebrities that make up my list are no longer living—George Burns, Sir Arthur Conan Doyle, Frederick Faust, Billie Holiday, Gene Krupa, John Lennon, Buddy Rich, Frank Sinatra, and John Steinbeck all now belong to the ages. Frankie Laine and Jerry Lewis, two more of my celebrity heroes, are still living.

Bravo to all heroes! You are special. And to those heroes still alive, may you always be kind to those who respect you and your work and look to you as their mentor. And may you always realize your life is blessed, because someone out there looks up to you.

AUTHOR'S NOTE

In 1997, while I was a newspaper writer, I rewrote a condensed version of an article detailing my first visit to meet singer Frankie Laine.

Initially, I wrote the story in 1995, shortly after I graduated from college and came to work for the publishing corporation that owned the newspaper I worked for. The story was originally published in a magazine designed for senior citizens. The article filled four pages of the tabloid-size magazine. Therefore, I thought it best to condense it for the newspaper article. Consequently, I received feedback from many readers, including Frankie, who very much enjoyed both the long and shortened versions.

Contrasting this enjoyment of the article, I received a letter from a person who was of the opinion I wrote and published my story for selfish promotion. This person obviously wasn't considerate enough to sign the letter or to even post a return address. Among other things, the letter berated my being shown in three of the article's photographs (two with Frankie Laine). In short, this person's assessment was that the story was written to glorify myself—the author.

Of course, I feel people are entitled to their opinions. That's as it should be. But because the letter was unsigned and mailed with no return address, I somehow felt my professionalism maliciously threatened. The letter made me feel gloomy. I couldn't understand why I was attacked. My intention was to relate the entertaining story of how a regular person (me) was lucky enough to be able to realize a quest. The story and circumstances are compelling. Many people were genuinely moved by it.

If someone were to perform an in-depth analysis, they would no doubt discover that anyone who strives to achieve something wonderful could be perceived as promoting themselves by "riding on someone else's coattails." We would not have movie stars, great writers, recording artists, comedians, doctors, teachers, and all the other wonderful people who make up our society if these people didn't strive to utilize the talents of others who were already established in order to learn and move onward and upward. In truth, they are not benefiting for selfish gain. These achievers are merely using established resources in order to attain for themselves the kind of worthwhile lives they strive for in order to give back something of themselves—to make a difference. Nobody can achieve in this world strictly on his or her own. I suspect even the writer of the letter at one point in time benefited either directly or indirectly from a successful forerunner.

My intent was to convey *my* story. Undoubtedly, people read my narrative because it was about Frankie Laine, not because it was about me. Again, that's as it should be. The magic of the article is the encounter between a celebrity and an admirer. I didn't write the story and exploit Frankie's fame for selfish purposes. My goal in detailing my first meeting with Frankie Laine was to enlighten readers to the majesty of being able to achieve a dream.

I wrote about the accomplishments of this great artist and detailed his unassuming nature. I conveyed Frankie's conviction that his fans are important to him. My account is both heartfelt and true; in my opinion, these two descriptive words are never a bad thing.

I composed *Reaching for a Star* with the same endearing approach. Among many other things, this book relates the story of the memoirist (me) who embarked on a quest and succeeded. It's about a mission that became reality, not by mere chance, but by a strong will, desire, and fortitude.

I know firsthand how difficult it is to become a successful working musician. By relating my struggle in the attempt to make a living playing music, I hope a realistic portrait emerges within the mind of the reader illustrating that music is an art form that is difficult to become successful at. Realizing the many passions lying within the effort to create a livelihood playing music demonstrates a perception that music is, indeed, an emotional art. This is important if the reader is to understand the strong endearing bond I have with Frankie Laine and Frankie's unique poignant vocal style.

The saga that unfolds within these pages revolves around a wonderful entertainer that has made my life better in many ways. Make no mistake, Frankie Laine is the star of this book. Mostly, this composition is my personal way of expressing gratitude to Frankie. If the reader finds enjoyment within its pages, this book will be a success.

The pictures of Frankie and me are included because, for the most part, this book is a chronicle of *my* times with Frankie Laine. It's not unlike my own personal scrapbook. This work details my life, my music, and my friendship with Frankie Laine. In many ways it is also a loving tribute to this great artist. I am honored I'm able to share my story with you. Good reading.

—Craig Cronbaugh

CHAPTER ONE
San Diego

First Time Together—Part I

A s I lay in the small bed and slowly opened my eyes, I suddenly recalled where I was. The early morning sun shone brightly and streamed wispily into my small room at the Veterans' YMCA, filling it with light and warmth. As I glanced at the brightness around me, my first thought was one of amusement because, after all, I *was* in sunny San Diego. Placing my hands behind my head I smiled thoughtfully—*Wow! Today's the day!*

The Journey

It was November 20, 1985. I arrived in San Diego the evening before after traveling from my home in Cedar Rapids, Iowa, by Greyhound bus. The trip of over two thousand miles took an exhausting two days and two nights. I disembarked dingy and travel weary. To make the trip even longer, my bus companions and I experienced a two-hour layover in Colorado due to a snowstorm.

I couldn't afford a more convenient mode of travel because I was really strapped for cash. Even though I was a full-time musician playing each night in Cedar Rapids, I was still far from rich. A drummer in a local band simply didn't make that much dough.

Without a doubt, though, the toughest thing I endured was saying good-bye to my little daughter, Latisha, at the bus depot. She was there with my girlfriend. Tishie was about to turn five years old, and even though I'd be back in time for her birthday, I still felt like I was deserting her. Tears filled my eyes as the bus began to move, and I watched her through the big bus window sadly waving good-bye to me.

The bus trip was long and boring. My hours were spent either looking out the window at the passing landscape, or reading the book of Sherlock Holmes stories I'd brought along. Each time we stopped to eat, I had precious little cash in my pocket to partake of anything substantial from the menus. It seemed we were stopping at the most expensive dives along the bus route. Many times coffee and maybe a doughnut were my only staples. But I had a quest. And come hell or high water, I was determined to see it through.

* * *

My family members are natives of Iowa. My parents lived in Urbana. I hadn't told them I was making this trip. Upon arriving at the Greyhound depot in San Diego, I went to a pay telephone and called home.

"Hello," Mom answered.

"Hi, this is Craig. I'll bet you'll never guess where I'm calling from," I teased.

Obviously thinking I was in town and pulling a prank, she replied, "Urbana?"

"No, San Diego, California!" I chirped excitedly.

All Mom could say was, "California!! What are you doing out there???"

After detailing my plans to Mom, while searching through the yellow pages and making phone calls, I failed to locate a cheap hotel. *Damn! Why didn't I bring more money?* Each hotel and motel I came across was way beyond my price range. I was scared. I needed to find a place to stay. I was tired, in a strange city, and had my luggage with me.

As soon as I arrived in San Diego, I was supposed to make another important phone call to set up the meeting for the following day. Temporarily, I gave up my search for a room and at the same pay telephone placed my call.

"You made the trip okay?" he inquired.

"Yes, but it was a long one," I answered. "I have a big problem," I went on. "All the hotels in this city are way too expensive for me; I didn't bring enough money."

"Where are you now?" I was asked.

I told him.

"That's near the Veterans' YMCA," he replied. "Since you're from out of state they'll let you stay there, and the rooms are inexpensive."

As I was fervently thanking him for the suggestion and directions, he went on to advise that I get a good night's rest and requested I call him the next morning around nine.

Unlike late autumn in Iowa, the air here was warm. Everywhere I looked the grass was green, the flowers in full bloom. People went about their business, seemingly unaware of their great weather.

I walked to the YMCA and checked in. Since this hotel was for veterans, I was asked to show some form of identification—proof that I was from out of state—in order to obtain a room for the night.

My room was tiny with only enough area to facilitate a small metal-frame bed and a place to keep my clothes. This was fine with me because it added a certain charm to my adventure. I didn't require a large comfortable room with a color television. I had a place to stay for the night and that's all that mattered. The solitary window in my room was sufficient, which, no doubt, would allow both the nighttime moonbeams and the morning sunlight into my temporary quarters.

Despite the trials and tribulations of the day, the evening was heavenly. I was dog-tired. Stretching out on my bed, I continued reading my Sherlock Holmes stories while smoking a bowl of my favorite pipe tobacco. *I am here. This quest is really going to happen!*

First Time Together—Part II

Both the sunshine and my excitement thoroughly awakened me, and I climbed out of bed. It was eight o'clock. Searching in my suitcase I found my shampoo and toothbrush. The YMCA didn't have in-room bathrooms. Instead, I walked down the long hallway to a community shower room.

The expansive floor in the men's shower room resembled the flooring in a barbershop with its black and white round tiles. Seemingly mocking privacy, each shower was open. I'd hoped for at least showers with surrounding stalls. The sinks were lined up in a row under a huge mirror, as if awaiting inspection. The only fixtures enclosed within the entire room were the toilets. I was extremely glad no one arrived to share in this tiled and porcelain bounty while I was there. The emptiness of this vast room was its only true salvation.

Being rather shy I didn't want to take a full shower, fearing that someone would come in and see me, so I did my best to quickly take a sponge bath, wash and dry my hair, and don my robe. Soon I was ready to go back to my room and get dressed. I put on my light blue dress slacks, best shirt, a navy blue vest, and matching suit coat. *Nothing but the best will do for today's meeting.*

When I was finished with my careful grooming, I packed up my suitcase along with another trunk-like suitcase, checked the contents of my briefcase, and sat back on the bed. I looked over the audiocassette recorder stored securely in my briefcase. I wanted it in perfect working order because I had plans to do a brief interview sometime during our visit. I also carefully inspected the four old ten-inch records and one seven-inch record I brought with me to be autographed. The fragile 78s suffered no damage from my long trip. I was somewhat worried about them surviving the journey, even though I had also carefully toted them in my briefcase. My briefcase never left my hands during the entire bus trip.

It was important that I obtain good photographs today. I felt a little concerned as I looked over the Fujica thirty-five-millimeter camera that my brother loaned me for the trip. I wasn't absolutely sure how to use the sensitive manual camera, but knew as long as I was convinced that everything through the viewfinder was in focus, the camera would likely not let me down.

Everything was ready. Now all I needed to do was make my morning phone call.

At almost nine o'clock I did a final search of my tiny room, grabbed my suitcases and briefcase, and looking, I'm sure, like Jerry Lewis in an old comedy movie, groped my way with my plethora of luggage to the elevator. When I arrived at the main floor, I asked the man behind the counter where I might find a pay telephone.

"How did you sleep?" I heard the voice at the other end of the line ask.

"Great," I answered.

"Good. Wait for me at the bottom of the steps in front of the hotel at twelve-thirty. I'll be waiting in my car to pick you up, and you'll accompany me on my rounds this afternoon," he informed me. *He's going to pick me up at twelve-thirty?! What in the hell am I going to do for the next three and a half hours?!*

I guess that in my naïve twenty-nine-year-old brain I thought my call was supposed to be the type of call you make when you're ready to be picked up. I gathered up my luggage and sauntered back to the elevator and, once again, back to my little room to wait.

I'd go crazy sitting in my room for so many hours. My belly was full of butterflies as it was. So, I decided to try to nap. I set my alarm for noon. Because I wore carefully sprayed collar-length hair—and the last thing

I needed was to have a flat-looking head all day—I became horizontal enough to fall into a sound sleep still wearing my suit.

The alarm rang seemingly minutes after I'd closed my eyes. Hurriedly, I reworked myself into a semblance of respectability. Luckily, my hairdo had survived my three hours of respite. Once again, I did the "too much luggage for one guy to carry" dance to the elevator and rode down to the main floor.

My stomach started growling as I entered the lobby and set down my luggage. Realization hit me in the gut. I was starved. I didn't have much time to eat, but I noticed a small lobby cafeteria was situated off to the side of the main counter. Even though I had only slightly more than ten dollars in my pocket, my return bus ticket was already paid for so I didn't worry too much. Checking my watch, I settled into a booth and ordered a sweet roll and coffee. Again, the prices were outrageously high—or maybe it just seemed so since I was practically broke. Even though I wolfed down the sweet roll and coffee, it still seemed like the small meal lasted for several minutes.

It was almost twelve-thirty. I grabbed my suitcases and ambled toward the hotel double doors ready to make my way to the assigned meeting location at the foot of the outside steps. As I approached the doors, I was close enough to look through the door windows when I was immediately blasted with two distinct emotions—fascination and trepidation. Of course, I recognized him immediately and couldn't wait to meet him, but momentarily hesitated. He was striding up the stairs from the outside toward the hotel doors, seemingly looking rather pissed. *Man, the last thing I need is to have him angry with me right from the start!*

In that moment I did my best to prepare myself for a heated outburst from him. He would want to know why I wasn't waiting outside as he had instructed on the phone. *Damn, because I wasn't waiting for him outside he had to find a parking space and walk into the hotel. Obviously, he had not wanted to do that or he wouldn't have directed me to be outside and waiting when he arrived. Not only has my meeting with him impinged on his day, but now I've also wasted his valuable time.*

To my utter astonishment, he simply smiled, held out his hand and very graciously said, "Hi, Craig. I'm Frankie Laine."

CHAPTER TWO

Beginnings

As well as I can recollect, I first became interested in Frankie Laine around 1970, when I was fourteen. Of course, I'd heard of him previous to that and knew he was a singer, but that was only because he was famous. I probably heard his name mentioned on the radio or on television in much the same way one hears about Yugoslavia at that age and realizes it's a country far away, but knows nothing more about it than that.

I was a big fan of the Beatles. It was because their drummer, Ringo Starr, mesmerized me that I began a keen interest in the drums. I first heard the Beatles sing "She Loves You" on the radio in 1963. That song was also featured on the first record by the Beatles I bought with money Grandpa Cronbaugh gave me.

In 1964, I acquired their record "I Want to Hold Your Hand" with the flip side featuring "I Saw Her Standing There." This record came complete with a sleeve that featured a photo of the Beatles—the famous one where

Paul McCartney is posing with a lit cigarette in his hand and all four are sporting their famous collarless jackets. The magic of their looks and the sound of their music were compelling. I still get goose bumps listening to their early recordings. Even now I sense the smell of our little overworked record player whenever I hear an early recording by the Beatles. The magic lingers on.

Upon listening to my copy of "She Loves You" at the tender age of seven, I definitely became smitten by the desire to become a musician, and I experienced the sheer magnetism and power of music.

I started taking drum lessons in the sixth grade and even joined the school band. By 1970, I had a sizeable collection of records and albums by the Beatles. Mom loved music. She brought music into my life, as well as into the lives of my younger siblings—two brothers and a sister.

Mom sang with her two sisters when they were kids. They even sang on a local radio show in Cedar Rapids. Consequently, Mom had many old 78s featuring musical artists that we kids played. Mom also loved listening to the radio throughout her daily housewife chores. During the 1960s, she listened to "top 40" stations that played the music that catered to the younger generation. That's how I first heard the Beatles, the Dave Clark Five, Gerry and the Pacemakers, and American music makers such as the Motown groups, Gene Pitney, Bobby Vee, and Bobby Vinton.

Later in the 1960s, Mom listened to the softer romantic and pop music stations that featured singers like Tony Bennett, Teresa Brewer, Perry Como, John Gary, Ella Fitzgerald, Steve Lawrence and Eydie Gormé, Patti Page, Frank Sinatra, Jerry Vale, and Andy Williams. Somewhere within this lineup, and in the middle of many other singers of this type, I'm sure

I heard Frankie Laine sing. I guess that's how I first became aware of his name when I was a kid.

When I was in my early teens, Ed Sullivan presented a retrospective of his popular television show. The show featured clips of performers who had appeared on his long-running musical variety show over the years. Because I knew he'd touch upon the Beatles and show a clip of them, I made sure I watched and even recorded the show with my audiocassette recorder by placing the microphone in front of the television speaker.

I guess I was a peculiar kid. I was a skinny, gawky, shy, pimply-faced teenager. I didn't get out much. Of course, I was further homebound because we lived on a farm, and I wasn't yet old enough to drive. I compensated by dreaming a lot. In my daydreams I was a good-looking, popular kid. I had dreams about girls. But most of all, I had aspirations about making my living by playing the drums.

Around this same time, I began listening to records featuring my drum idols Gene Krupa and Buddy Rich. I emulated them. They were so cool. As a result, I began playing their albums. This drummer idol worship introduced me to a different type of music—jazz. While other kids my age were digging rock and roll, I was listening to music utilizing brass and woodwinds. I read about different popular drummers of the past. My admiration of this type of music further led to an interest in listening to records by many of the old big bands.

I began picturing myself in a big band that played each night in big fancy dance halls. Many of the big band records I listened to featured vocalists. I enjoyed this type of studious melodic singing. In my mind I was a famous drummer. I lived vicariously through my drummer idols.

This mindset gave me courage whenever I was among my peers in school. While my fellow students were seeing me as a dork, I was envisioning myself as an actor in a movie playing the part of either a singer resembling a young John Lennon or a famous drummer who was cool and played as well as Gene Krupa or Buddy Rich. My heroes helped me get through those difficult and awkward times.

After the Ed Sullivan retrospective aired, I was listening to the cassette tape I'd recorded and heard the coolest singer I'd ever heard in my life. That singer, Johnnie Ray, absolutely floored me. His clip on the program was a short treatment of his popular song "Cry." This little segment absolutely blew me away! I didn't know this singer's name until I played my audio of this clip for Dad, asking if he knew who this singer was. "That's Johnnie Ray," Dad answered after hearing the clip. "He had that one hit song and then faded away. I don't know what ever happened to him." (I soon discovered that Johnnie Ray had several big hit records during his career.)

Well, this sealed it for me. There was something about being an elusive singer with such a neat song that intrigued me. *Wow! A legend who just vanished into the sunset.* I hadn't paid much attention, but a clip or two after Johnnie Ray, a rugged male singer was featured singing the staccato ending: *"Jez-e-bel, Jez-e-bel, Jez . . e . . bel!!"*

When Dad heard this he proclaimed, "That's Frankie Laine—he was always my favorite singer."

Frankie Laine—this name sounded familiar. The audio clip featuring Frankie began to interest me. It was unique and full of bravado. I soon found myself enchanted. Some of this fascination was no doubt due to Dad telling me that Frankie Laine was his favorite singer. It's human nature. When a parent suggests a favorite thing to their child at that tender age, it automatically becomes the child's favorite. That's how it is. It's simply written in the stars.

By the early 1970s, the nostalgia craze was beginning to happen. It began with a revival in the interest of music from the 1950s. The public began watching television advertising featuring albums hosting a compilation of musical groups from the 1950s. I bought one of these album sets. It presented groups like the Crew Cuts, the Platters, and almost all the old hits my parents remembered from their youth.

I excitedly sought records by both Johnnie Ray and Frankie Laine in the record stores. I knew there must be rereleased hits out there. I found a *Johnnie Ray's Greatest Hits* album and a *Frankie Laine's Greatest Hits* album on the same day in the same record store. Johnnie Ray's album included "Cry," and Frankie Laine's album featured "Jezebel."

Between listening to the Beatles and jazz drummers, I also played the Johnnie Ray and Frankie Laine albums. I was enthralled while listening to these great singers. Even though the recordings were already almost twenty years old, to me they seemed so fresh—so alive. I soon came to the realization that this is the impact these famed singers and their songs must have originally had on millions of people around the world. Each song I played on these albums seemed better than the one before. It was sheer joy to listen to both "Cry" and "Jezebel" in their studio quality perfection— "electronically enhanced for stereo," of course.

I brought out my Frankie Laine *Greatest Hits* album one evening while we had company over and played it on my parents' stereo in the living room. My dad spoke up and said, "Listen to that orchestra. Frankie Laine sang with only the best musicians." Coming from Dad, this really impressed me, during this, my impressionable age. Looking back, there's no doubt in my mind that Dad's constant affirmation of Frankie Laine's music had much to do with the beginnings of the magic and sheer wonder of Frankie Laine's sound etching itself into my young brain.

For what it's worth, I analyzed the arts in a most unorthodox way. I loved dreaming and imagining. For example, I once read a biography on the great humorist Will Rogers. While looking at an old photograph of him in the book, I imagined what life was like just outside the door at the time that picture was taken. *Did the food taste the same as it does now? What was happening in the news that day?*

I always had a peculiar and introspective way of envisioning certain things. If I saw a photo in a book or watched a scene in a movie, I'd often reflect beyond the representation. One of the most famous movie scenes in the history of the motion picture is the scene during the first few moments of the movie *The Wizard of Oz* where Judy Garland, as Dorothy, sings "Over the Rainbow." As she sings, she is shown on the screen grasping the metal spokes of an old-fashioned, horse-driven piece of farm machinery. A little later in the same scene her dog, Toto, jumps up onto the metal seat. This prop for the movie looks very authentic. Most likely, it was a genuine piece of machinery once actually used by some long-gone farmer during some long-lost decade, years before the movie was filmed. I wondered what the farmer would have thought then had he known that one day his metal tool-of-the-trade would become a part of movie history.

I believe this thought process, whether normal or abnormal, is why I am able to transcend beyond a particular artist's work and ultimately discover that artist's passion. I don't enjoy the work merely for what it represents on the surface, but also the thought processes behind it.

I began playing in a band on weekends when I was fourteen. My desire was to play drums in a jazz or swing band or orchestra, but in the early 1970s the only bands playing for dances in bars and clubs predominantly performed country music. For the most part, I was content in the knowledge that at least I was drumming in a band. This musical group played in Cedar Rapids—about twenty-five miles from where I lived. The band members were older and took turns picking me up at home and returning me in the wee hours of the morning, after the gigs. It was great fun, and I made enough money to pay for my own schoolbooks and lunch tickets. Partially paying my way in school by playing music was a great source of pride for me. It reinforced the justification of playing music not only for me, but also for my parents.

I rapidly became a fan of most of the music and styles of the 1950s. I delighted in seeing the photographs of my parents when they were married in 1954. The black and white pictures were able to create a feeling of the era. My mind explored them, in much the same way an artist delves into his painting. This dramatic look transported me into an era that no longer existed. These pictures seemed like a time portal that I stepped into. I noticed the youth and beauty of my parents and grandparents. Oh, to be able to be there in the pictures—to listen to the music—to drive the neat-looking cars!

I especially loved the cars. As a kid I had always wanted a Model A Ford. My grandpa used to tell me stories of his youth and they were resplendent with the old cars. I thought nothing could be neater than to drive one of those funny-looking automobiles—perhaps pretending that I was actually living in this bygone era. Later, I delighted in the big tank-like cars of the 1940s. But after being introduced to the music of the 1950s, I began to fall in love with that decade's shiny-chromed, single-headlight beauties.

As it turned out, my first car was a 1956 Ford four-door sedan. The car was my age! I was fifteen, but I couldn't pass up the opportunity to buy this car when I noticed it for sale on the car lot in town. The car cost less than one hundred dollars and was a rust bucket, but I loved it. I used to wash it, wax it, and bought all kinds of car things for it such as gas pedal and brake pedal covers, floor mats, and a steering wheel cover. I even installed all kinds of extra instrument panel gauges under the dash. My car was resplendent with gadgets—including a genuine old-fashion-sounding *ah-ooh-gah* horn. While observing me totally enthralled with fixing up my car, Grandpa Cronbaugh used to chuckle and say, "Craig can't drive it yet, but he can 'pet' it."

* * *

I yearned to experience more Frankie Laine music. One day, while on a shopping trip with Mom, I searched the record store and bought two Frankie Laine albums that were released later in his career, in the early 1960s. These albums contained songs previously available on other records. One album was featured on the Columbia Records reissue label, Harmony Records, and the other on Pickwick, a Capitol label reissue. Surprisingly, these two collections were totally unlike the Frankie Laine compilation of old hit songs I was rapidly wearing out. Furthermore, I discovered that these two albums seemed quite different in both style and orchestration. The Harmony album was made up of cowboy songs. The Pickwick set featured an orchestrated pop style along with overtones of inspirational music. Even though I loved both albums, I was especially intrigued with the cowboy songs.

I couldn't believe my ears. I rapidly became convinced nobody could sing cowboy songs with as much style and feeling as Frankie Laine. His sound was that of a manly cowboy, singing with feeling and integrity. Singer and orchestration meshed flawlessly. This wasn't simply a singer singing—this was a singer *feeling* each word. In addition to the overall unmatched vocal performance, Frankie topped off each song with amazing tone, interpretation, and form. In this album, I rediscovered the song "Rawhide." I'd definitely heard that song before. I remember hearing that on television as a child. *Is this when I first also heard the name "Frankie Laine"?* I guess I'll never know for sure. One thing I did know, however, was that I had discovered Frankie Laine for myself. I was familiarizing myself with his music, and this would be the start of my own personal study of Frankie Laine's art.

Early in 1972, two concerts rekindled my fire for jazz and big band music. My school band instructor acquired tickets to attend a Stan Kenton concert at an Iowa college. He announced this to the entire band class, and I was anxious to go. My band instructor was able to generate an interest in only one other kid a couple of grades ahead of me.

As luck would have it, I didn't have to find my own transportation to the event. The band instructor was a young bachelor and didn't have anything preventing him from driving all three of us to the concert.

Kenton's band was astounding! Before the first set was finished, his trumpet players blew out a speaker from the sheer velocity of their bravado performance into the on-stage microphone. During intermission, I meandered up to the piano and chatted with Kenton. He was very nice and asked me what school I attended. Before the start of the concert, I'd purchased one of his albums. He now cordially autographed it for me. (Years later I added to my collection a videotape copy of Frankie Laine performing on a Stan Kenton television show in 1955.)

In April, my school band instructor, once again, announced he could get tickets to a live concert. This time the event would feature famed jazz drummer Buddy Rich. The performance would take place at Upper Iowa College in Fayette. I was ecstatic! There's no way I'd miss this concert. Like he did for the Stan Kenton show, my band instructor took me to see Buddy Rich. He didn't particularly want to go, but I talked him into it. There was no way I could pass up seeing my drummer idol!

As it turned out, my band instructor and I were the only ones who went from my school. It was very foggy the night of the concert. I truly feared for my life because visibility was bad, and my youthful life was totally at the mercy of my band instructor who was, to say the least, a young and crazy driver. Later that night at the concert, Buddy even alluded to the fog during his band's intermission. Grabbing the stage microphone, Buddy said to the audience, "I thank you for coming out tonight. I appreciate the fact that it was difficult. I wouldn't come out to see *me* on a night like this! And you know how I feel about *me!!*"

Buddy Rich simply fascinated me. His band was the best. Just prior to the start of the concert, I obtained Buddy's autograph on a drumhead I had brought along just for that purpose. I even shook hands with him! Buddy's face was well-tanned and lined with wrinkles. I was surprised he looked so old up close. To me, his facial features resembled that of an ancient Indian. He wore his hair the same length as the Beatles in their early days and was dressed in slacks and a suit coat.

Just before the big band began performing, management granted permission for several members of the audience to move closer and sit on the floor directly in front of the stage. I sat directly in front of and below Buddy and his drums. For me, it was a night never to be forgotten.

I continued to play in bands and about the time I was old enough to acquire my driver's license, in July 1972, I graduated to a better band. In addition to country music, this band also featured rock and roll.

Later that summer, a friend and I drove to the Great Jones County Fair in Monticello, Iowa, to see singer Bobby Vinton. Bobby was always a favorite singer of mine. I have the type of voice that can mimic his. Because of this, I enjoyed singing along with his records.

After the show, I received Bobby's autograph, took a picture of him, and even spoke to him briefly.

I also saw the Carpenters in person in October 1972. They performed in Waterloo, Iowa. By seeing these famous people in person, and sometimes even shaking hands or speaking to them, I was becoming aware this was creating an open invitation for the celebrity bug to begin biting me.

In 1973, I briefly attended a Duke Ellington Concert at Hancher Auditorium in Iowa City. A school friend went with me, and I drove us to Iowa City. Once there and only a short distance from Hancher, I started to turn to the left and failed to see an approaching car racing through a green light, its driver obviously trying to make it through before it turned. The woman driving didn't make it. Even though I had a green light, I didn't have a green arrow; therefore, I was supposed to yield to approaching traffic. What transpired seemed in slow motion. Perhaps I had the concert on my mind. Anyway, our cars collided nearly head-on. The woman and, to my further dismay, her little girl were taken to the hospital. Luckily, they were not seriously injured and later released.

My companion and I were unhurt—only a bit shaken. After dealing with the police and having my car towed to a storage lot, I telephoned Mom and Dad to explain what had happened and ask them to drive to Iowa City to pick us up.

My friend and I walked to Hancher and saw Duke Ellington. We listened to a couple of songs performed by Ellington and his band before leaving the auditorium and walking to the rendezvous point where Mom and Dad were to meet us and take us home. The day turned out to be not at all like I had expected.

I drove to Drake University in Des Moines to see my second live Buddy Rich concert on February 8, 1974. Even though I didn't get as close to the stage as I did the first time I saw Buddy and his orchestra, this genius drummer amazed me nonetheless.

By the time I graduated from high school in 1974, I drove a 1965 Plymouth and hauled my own drums to my weekend gigs. My goal was to play full time and make my living by playing music.

One evening, a few days after graduation, I drove to a popular dance hall in Keystone, Iowa, and watched and listened to famed bandleader Harry James perform with his orchestra.

Before the show—which was also a dance—began, James' autograph was forthcoming, and I shook his hand. He was not at all happy about this because I was apparently honing in on his "warm-up" time before the performance. His adversity was all too plain. In fact, he actually informed me that I was bothering him while he was warming up. This was my first one-on-one contact with a famous person who was less than cordial.

Later that evening I chatted with James' drummer, Les DeMerle, who was quite nice. In a strange way, I thought it fascinating that James was not cordial. It seemed odd, and I can't really explain it, but I've always felt a certain romanticism regarding someone famous being nice on television or in the movies, only to be unpleasant in person. Many stars have the reputation of being less than affable when it comes to individual contact with their fans. I always considered this assuming attitude—for whatever reason—kind of cool. This was my opinion, that is, until I had an abrupt personal encounter with a famous person the following year.

Early in 1975, I auditioned and was chosen to be the drummer in a professional band that performed, on average, three nights each week in Cedar Rapids. This band featured a variety of music, and I found myself happily playing in a band that produced a good sound. Three months before I started with this band, the members recorded an album in Nashville.

In order to be independent and have my own apartment, I worked many odd jobs in addition to playing at night. At this juncture, I swept out railroad boxcars each morning for a paltry sum.

During 1975, I saw many of my favorite performers live. I saw Chubby Checker, Gary Lewis, Rick Nelson, and Bobby Vee. Rick Nelson was performing at an outdoor fair, so I wasn't able to get too close.

That spring, Bobby Vee, Gary Lewis, and Chubby Checker were at the Ramada Inn in Cedar Rapids. Bobby Vee appeared there in April. After his performance, I spoke to Bobby briefly, shook his hand, and received a personal autograph. He was very nice. Gary Lewis performed there in May. I also talked with Gary Lewis after his show. When asked, he cordially provided me with an autograph. Chubby Checker held a concert there in June. He made himself conveniently unavailable after his performance, but did invite people toward the stage to receive his "John Hancock" just before ending his show. Of course, I was one who got his autograph this way.

My apartment roommate, Danny Aarhus, who was also the lead guitarist in the band I was currently in, had tagged along with me to partake in the concert by Gary Lewis and the Playboys. While I chatted with Gary, Danny struck up a conversation with Gary's guitar player. Subsequently, Danny was invited up to the band's hotel room for a party. Since we came to the show together, we both went upstairs to the band's room. Everyone in the band sat around talking, drinking, and smoking. Suddenly, the door to the adjacent room opened and in walked a shirtless Gary Lewis! He stayed and chatted a bit, then left. Shortly thereafter, and not wanting to overstay our welcome, Danny and I left. To be sure, this experience was one of my luckier excursions.

I revered Gary Lewis and the Playboys almost as long as I had the Beatles. Gary Lewis is the son of one of my favorite comedians—Jerry Lewis. As a kid, I watched all the old Dean Martin and Jerry Lewis movies on television. Mom loved this popular entertainment duo. I absolutely adore Jerry Lewis. Here I was, actually spending time within the world of his son, Gary! I was really psyched! Gary was extremely nice to me. He was totally unpretentious. I'd have to say that up to this point in my life, Gary Lewis was the one entertainer who renewed my faith in celebrity benevolence. He treated me with kindness and respect, thus rekindling my belief that there are, indeed, famous people who are polite to the individuals who idolize them. This was a far cry from my brush with Buddy Rich in November.

The band that Danny and I were in that year mostly played Wednesday nights and weekends. Danny and I lived in a rental house in Cedar Rapids that cost over two hundred dollars a month. We needed to make more money. By pooling a couple of our musician friends, we formed our own little band to play Tuesdays and Thursdays at one of the clubs our regular band booked. We booked for a cut-rate price so the clubs wouldn't turn us down. This band was unsuccessful because we didn't get paid much, and we couldn't seem to schedule rehearsals with the other musicians. Nobody wanted to put forth an effort when they were only making peanuts. As a result, we lacked a professional sound, and everybody soon lost interest in the whole project.

During a break one night in the summer of 1975, while we were playing at a club with our regular band, Danny and I met a man who was a top foreman for a local roofing company. We ended up going with his entourage to his girlfriend's house to party after the gig. As the party progressed, this man offered Danny and me a job with the roofing company. The company specialized in repairing and restoring flat roofs on commercial buildings.

Desperate for a better financial income, Danny and I began working with the roofing crew the following Monday. The shift started before sunup so the crew could finish early in the afternoon before it got too hot. This was important because the tar that is used to tar the roofs had to be heated to five hundred degrees and hauled up to the roofs in five-gallon buckets. Then, once on top of each roof the tar had to be mopped onto each roof. Because of the heat of the tar and the heat of the Iowa summer sun, the crewmen wisely decided they'd rather get up earlier in the morning and have their eight hours in before it got unbearably hot.

Of course, Danny and I were relegated to the lowest position in the crew. Unfortunately for us, we were assigned to a foreman who hated musicians. He disliked Danny in particular. He also despised me. Not only was I a musician, but I was also Danny's friend. We later discovered this grudge was born from a rather infamous story unfortunately involving Danny. According to the tale, Danny once dated this guy's sister and eventually unceremoniously dumped her. Whether fact or fiction, this story apparently carried enough clout to ensure our days were pure hell on earth working with this crew.

Some days Danny and I had to shovel pea gravel into a conveyor that took it to the top of each roof. One day I was instructed to perform this particular task for the entire shift. There happened to be sixteen tons of gravel in a pile on the ground that I scooped into the conveyer. Pea gravel is extremely heavy, and it doesn't take much to add up to a substantial, backbreaking weight. I shoveled the whole pile that day. I recall thinking that I loaded sixteen tons, like the lyrics in my Frankie Laine recording "Sixteen Tons." I knew what it felt like to do this at age nineteen. We also had to carry five-gallon buckets of this gravel.

As far as I was concerned, the worst task associated with this ungodly job was tearing "pitch," or chunks of the old hard tar, packed tight with old gravel, off the roofs. The crew broke up these sections of pitch with a straight crowbar, and we had to tear them off, lift the pieces up, and carry them to the edge of each roof and fling them onto the truck bed below. All the while we toiled, the foreman stood over us like a drill sergeant and angrily bawled us out, demanding that we work faster or we'd be fired.

Danny and I were soaked with sweat, sore, and dog-tired by the end of each day. "Why is the foreman riding us?" we asked the man who hired us. As an answer, he promised to speak with this musician-hating foreman and ask him to "lighten up." Judging by subsequent treatment at the hands of our foreman, however, I doubt if an intervention ever happened.

Of course, three days each week were especially hell on earth. Those days included Wednesdays and Fridays, because we had to summon up the strength and stamina to play in the band those evenings, and Thursday morning, because we'd have to get up early and go to work after playing the night before. Danny and I stuck out this drudgery for a few weeks before finally giving up and quitting. The money was good, but we wanted to live, not die of undue exhaustion.

* * *

I drove to Rock Island, Illinois, in mid-November to, once again, see a live Buddy Rich concert. Buddy was performing at the Rock Island Fieldhouse. The concert was wonderful, and I'd never heard Buddy's band in better form.

During the band's intermission, after his usual audience *shtick* on the microphone, Buddy walked to the corner of the stage to sit and sign autographs. I bought one of the program booklets at the door and wanted Buddy to autograph a picture in the booklet. The picture featured him as a small child billed as "Traps, the Drum Wonder."

For some inexplicable reason, the people in the autograph line seemed crazed. This was possibly due to the high velocity of the concert, which had everybody energized, coupled with the frenzied realization that these fans must have felt in being literally within reach of the star drummer. The crowd kept trying to swarm Buddy as he was signing autographs. This undoubtedly put him in a rather foul mood. At one point he actually forcefully informed the horde, "If everyone doesn't get back so I can have some air, I'm not signing any more autographs!" The group retreated a bit and Buddy, seemingly satisfied, went on hastily signing.

Finally, it was my turn, and I received my autograph on the picture in the booklet, then moved away from the line of autograph seekers. I desperately wanted to ask Buddy a question and figured this was my one and only chance to do so. Somehow I drew up enough nerve. I don't know where my courage came from, but I was bent on doing it no matter what.

The timing was in all probability wrong given Buddy's angry outburst at those who wanted an autograph moments before, but, nonetheless, I sat beside him on the stage.

Buddy was still intent on fervently signing autographs. Sucking in my breath and facing him I asked, "Buddy, what do you think of the soul groups that feature a horn section such as Tower of Power?"

This musical group was one of my favorites. Buddy, still signing away and not looking up, shook his head back and forth. I was about to counter with, *"Oh, you don't like them?"* but never got the chance.

Suddenly, while still signing autographs, Buddy angrily hissed, "Don't ask me anything! I'm not here to answer any goddamn questions!"

I was devastated. *What just happened?!* I couldn't see straight. I was close to tears. My head was spinning. I was only nineteen years old—still just a big kid—and my drummer idol had just crushed me with his retort. I was taken completely off guard. I continued to love Buddy Rich and his drumming, but this little tirade would never be forgotten and troubled me for a long time.

* * *

As far as I was concerned, there had to be a way of earning a living by utilizing my craft. That December I made up my mind to seek out full-time employment in a band in Chicago. In Cedar Rapids, most nightclubs didn't book bands every night of the week. In Chicago, a musician could make a living.

I always hoped to seek my fortune in San Francisco after hearing stories about how Danny played in a successful band there a couple of years earlier—on a full-time basis. As fate would have it, Danny came back once to visit friends in Cedar Rapids and ended up wrecking his car. Somehow he was unable to get out of the car after the accident. Tragically, since the car engine continued running, he breathed in a lot of carbon monoxide, which destroyed numerous brain cells. Even though Danny was still a darned good guitarist after the accident, he had to leave his gig in San Francisco for reasons he never explained. Perhaps it was because of his short-term memory loss—a direct result of his accident. It was always quite evident that Danny possessed a terrible memory. Many times when we'd be lounging around at home he'd ask me a question, which I'd answer, then he would ask the same question a short time later. Even though I always considered Danny a bit eccentric, he became my personal musical mentor. Upon learning of his car accident, I understood why he was a bit different, although it never bothered me in the least.

Danny lived for the moment. If the moment didn't include washing his hair—no problem, he simply carried out most of his daily routines sporting long, thinning, greasy-looking hair. He also wore a mustache, which, at best, could be described as untrimmed. Danny's clothes consisted of a couple of shirts and the pairs of pants from the three different leisure suits we wore in the band. He was definitely one of a kind.

One night after a band gig, Danny and I talked for a long while about each other's lives. Danny became serious as he recounted his San Francisco story to me. "Craig, I used to be so happy I couldn't even get to sleep when I went to bed," he disclosed. "I'd lie there and think about the gig the next night and how much fun it was going to be."

He alluded to the money. "I used to have a bankroll in my pockets everywhere I went," he recalled.

While Danny was with this band they recorded a two-sided demo record for Warner Brothers Records. This amazed me. I was more determined than ever with the notion of making my living as a full-time drummer in a band.

Danny would tempt me by saying, "Craig, if you go to San Francisco, you can make a good living playing every night. Maybe someday we can go there together and give it a try."

I needed money and was committed to fulfilling my dream. *I must go to San Francisco.* It was with this mindset that I spoke my piece to my Uncle Bob during our family Thanksgiving get-together. My mom's kid brother is only around eight years my senior and a childhood favorite of mine. Bob played guitar and was in bands during his school years and beyond. I'll always remember what he said to me that day, "Craig, why don't you go to Chicago? It's closer, and besides, it's larger than San Francisco."

From that moment on, I set my sights on Chicago. I began to see myself as another Gene Krupa. Gene played in Chicago many times. I read in a famous jazz magazine, while I was still in school, that Gene is buried in a cemetery in Calumet City, a suburb of Chicago.

That December, just before Christmas, I asked Danny if he wanted to go with me to Chicago. I informed him I was going to seek out and find a full-time band job there and play the drums each night of the week. Danny agreed to come along with me. One thing I appreciated about Danny was that he was always willing to be there for me when I needed him. I guess it worked both ways because I had to pick up the tab for his share of our rent on more than one occasion. At any rate, my family was relieved to know that I wasn't going to the big city alone. It was also a plus for them that Danny was a few years older than me. Somehow that made it less frightening for my family. Without a doubt, it also made it less scary for me. Danny had lived in San Francisco, so he knew how to handle himself in a big city. Up until then, the biggest city I had ever spent time in was Des Moines.

At breakfast after a gig early one morning, I informed the rest of my fellow band members that I was headed for Chicago. I excitedly proclaimed that my goal was to find a job in a band playing drums every night of the week. Thankfully, Danny was absent from this bashing occasion, where each of the other band members took their turns berating my news. I guess in their eyes I was stupid for even considering going to Chicago, and even more foolish to think I could land a full-time band gig. They really let me have it. I don't know why. They were pretty malicious about the whole affair. In the early hours of this particular morning, in a rather chivalrous way, I took every discouraging word the other band members threw at me without shame.

A few days later, Danny and I set off for Chicago. I was extremely impressed with the Windy City. As darkness approached, all the trees and bushes in the city were emblazoned with white Christmas lights literally as far as the eye could see. The skyline was fabulous and beautiful lit up against the night sky. Seemingly a magical haze swept over the cityscape at night, giving it an enchanting look. It seemed to mirror the effect of watching a close-up of a beautiful movie starlet of the 1940s, filmed in soft focus. I was totally mesmerized.

That evening Danny and I visited club after club and listened to bands. In every club I asked the bandleader if he needed a new drummer or knew of any bands that might be looking for a drummer. Time and time again we were unsuccessful in fulfilling this quest of mine. To make matters worse, a taxicab driver pulled up to a curb while we were walking down the sidewalk and rolled down his window. "Hey, you guys . . . hop in. I'll take you to a real swingin' nightclub for half price."

I was naïve, to be sure, but Danny displayed uncharacteristic naïveté too, because we both took the taxicab driver at his word and not only were stiffed for a hefty fare, but the promised "swingin' nightclub" turned out to be a dull, smoky, two-bit strip joint.

Later, Danny and I walked onward to Chicago's famous Rush Street. We stopped in at a quaint club called Country on Rush. A barker bombastically greeted us and ushered us inside. Within this red, darkly lit club a country rock trio was playing in an area behind a small stage. On the stage a woman danced to their music while provocatively taking her clothes off. This was pretty ritzy stuff for me—a mere baby at nineteen. Danny and I seated ourselves at a side table. Almost immediately a pretty lass sat down beside me and another settled in next to Danny. My new "friend" snuggled up to me and seemed fascinated with every word I spoke. I couldn't believe this! *I am a sensation!* Never before had a female seemed so spellbound with me.

"I am a musician," I said.

"Oh my," she breathed, snuggling closer.

"I'm from Iowa," I gallantly decreed.

Soon thereafter she did something totally unexpected. Reaching out she rubbed my leg as she looked dreamily into my eyes as if thinking, *You're so goddamn fascinating you big hunk of man—tell me more . . . .*

"Would you care to buy the lady a drink?" asked an older woman, dressed in tight, very short shorts who suddenly appeared holding a drink tray. This query seemed to break my spell, as I nodded. Somehow I reclaimed my composure. Not an easy task for a young man in this particular circumstance.

"Would you ask the leader of the band if he needs a new drummer or knows of anyone looking?" I timidly asked my new friend.

"Sure," she answered, to my delight.

She tottered up to the stage after the band finished the song they were playing, and I watched her talk to the bandleader, who suddenly looked my way.

As soon as the band took a break, the bandleader walked over to where I was sitting and introduced himself. "Hello. I'm Steve Williams. I understand you're looking for a drumming job."

I shook his hand and nodded, introducing myself at the same time. "Well, Craig," Steve continued, "it just so happens I'm looking for a drummer. Our current drummer is leaving soon. Do you want to sit in?" *My God! This is too good to be true!*

"You bet!" I excitedly exclaimed.

Steve was tall and sported a short-brimmed cowboy-type hat. A small mustache appeared over his thin lips. His demeanor was straightforward. Steve's best attribute was definitely exhibited on the stage with a voice that was wonderful, full of feeling, and executed with a warm tone.

When the next set began, I was up there with the band. The songs they played were songs I knew, so I was very confident. Without a doubt, I knew I was a much better player than the drummer I'd just heard. After the second song, Steve turned around and said four magic words to me—"You got the job." Then he spoke into the microphone, "How about a nice hand for Craig for sitting in with us." That was my cue to get up and let their drummer resume, so I strode back to the table in an excited daze.

"He offered me a job with them, Danny!" Danny couldn't believe my luck. He wasn't the only one.

During the next band break, Steve again sauntered over to our table and informed me that he was impressed with my playing. With a very matter-of-fact delivery, Steve said, "If you would like the job drumming for my band, it's yours for as long as you want it. You'll play seven nights a week, and I'll pay you two hundred twenty-five dollars a week."

I informed Steve I would take him up on his offer, but couldn't start until the first Sunday in January. I was committed to playing a big New Year's Eve gig with my present band in Iowa. Besides, I was slated to make one hundred sixty-six dollars for playing only four hours, and I required this money to help facilitate my move to Chicago.

"I'll expect you to be here and start on that date then," Steve answered.

For the rest of the night I was bathed in a feeling of contentment and bliss, much the same way a child feels on Christmas Eve. My blond gal buddy eventually made her way back over to my table, this time addressing me in a more business-like voice totally unlike the cooing earlier in the evening. "I heard you'll be working with us here. Congratulations."

Before we left Country on Rush that night, I discovered from Steve that I would play at the club Sunday through Thursday nights from nine until three the following morning. The band would perform musical sets behind girls dancing and stripping to our music. Then, on Friday and Saturday nights, we would play from nine-thirty until five-thirty the next morning at another club located in the Chicago suburb of Stone Park.

Upon leaving the club, Steve said something to me that caused my skin to crawl. "I'll expect you to be here on the date we agreed upon. Don't make me have to send some of my boys to Iowa to look for you." There was no mirth in the tone of his voice.

* * *

Everyone back home was excited. No one could believe that I ventured to Chicago on a quest to find full-time work drumming for a band and accomplished just that. I couldn't even believe it. I think Danny was envious, because during the last few gigs that I worked with him, he seemed very depressed. One of the clearest images I have of Danny was after we played our New Year's Eve gig and were paid. I went to find Danny and saw him sitting alone at a table with several beers in front of him, guzzling each as fast as he could, all the while clenching what was left of his one hundred sixty-six dollars in his hand. It was both amusing and sad at the same time.

Danny had a dark side. Earlier that year, I drove him to a doctor's appointment. He asked me to drive him because his car broke down the day before. As we took off for downtown, Danny informed me that his father had committed suicide. I knew his father had died several years prior, now I was learning how. After telling me this, Danny had a nervous breakdown in my car while I was driving. He started bawling relentlessly, and in between sobs I learned he had taken an overdose of pills because he wanted to die. It's a good thing we were headed for a doctor. My friend was really messed up. At nineteen, I didn't know how to react to him during this crisis in his life. It was scary.

* * *

To prepare for my new Chicago career, I equipped my drums with new heads, bought two new pairs of drumsticks, and joined Cedar Rapids Local 137 of the American Federation of Musicians. I packed my old van with all my worldly possessions and was finally ready for my trip into the unknown.

My vehicle was a 1965 Ford Econoline van. It was once owned by a telephone company. Now it uncaringly sported a sanded white area where the former logo used to be displayed. The faded-red exterior resembled the color of a half-ripe tomato.

The taillights were round and built flatly into the van's rear. One of the back rear corners under the taillight had once been smashed. A pool of hardened and never-sanded pink body filler, closely resembling frosting on a cake, unsuccessfully concealed the deformity. My van didn't look like much, but it was reliable transportation.

On the morning of Sunday, January 4, 1976, I said a tearful good-bye to Mom, Dad, my brothers, and my sister and set out for Cedar Rapids. It was clear and extremely cold. I dressed in insulated long underwear, many layers of warm clothes, and topped it all off with insulated coveralls. Dressing warm was a necessity because the heater in my van was less than adequate. After a short stop in Cedar Rapids, I left my friends behind and began the over two-hundred-fifty-mile trek to Chicago.

It was bitter cold and dark when I reached Chicago. My feet were numb. My van's small heater was almost useless. Because I had played the Friday and Saturday nights before, I was tired both physically and emotionally.

I spoke previously with Steve on the phone a few times upon returning to Iowa—in preparation for my trip. He gave me detailed instructions to his house in the suburbs. I arrived at his house around six o'clock. He introduced me to his wife. A baby daughter completed his family. While there, I grabbed a bite to eat, cleaned and dressed for my first gig, and was instructed by Steve to follow him to the club. I followed his car close behind in my van. I didn't want to lose him in traffic. Upon arriving on Rush Street, Steve pulled into a small parking lot, and we left our vehicles to the attendant. I unloaded all my drums and carried them to the club. Even though I was extremely tired and the weather was wintry cold, I was jubilant to be starting my new career.

The first week was great. One night as I was walking to the club from the parking lot, two prostitutes almost ran me down while running toward me, a policeman in hot pursuit. *This is the big city!* I smiled to myself. *I am here! Yes, I am here!*

At first, I stayed with Steve and his small family. Later, I bunked at the apartment of one of the dancing girls who worked at the club. Steve arranged this. My instructions were to stay with her until I found my own place to live. Additionally, I was expected to share expenses and, most importantly, not have anything to do with her sexually.

I was a skinny, bespectacled, naïve kid, so I don't think this young lady figured she was in imminent danger of my throwing myself at her. Furthermore, I really didn't have to worry about her thinking I was some kind of Romeo that she would attack. Therefore, upon the realization of knowing where I stood in this situation, I slept rather contentedly on the floor in her living room. Her cat, Magoo, regarded me with the utmost disinterest.

This platonic relationship did nothing to alleviate her boyfriend's dislike of this living arrangement. I listened to them argue about it more than once as I lay on the floor in my makeshift bed. Bottom line: I needed to find my own place as soon as possible.

A couple of weeks after moving in with my female roommate, I found my own apartment. Thus, I began a routine I would follow from January through May 1976.

I played seven nights each week with no time off. The hours were long for playing music. Usually, big-time musicians play a couple of hours each night. We were playing forty-six hours a week.

The winter of 1976 was one of the coldest winters I'd experienced. My van didn't seem to want to start most of the time after sitting for several hours in the rental parking lot near the club until I finished playing. I remedied this by carrying an old beat-up five-gallon gas can in my van with just enough gas in it to make a "swish" sound when picked up. My van's engine was housed snuggly in between the bucket seats inside the cab. This made for easy access to the six-cylinder workhorse. I merely lifted up the housing, removed the air cleaner, opened the choke on the carburetor, and poured a small dribble of gas down its throat. After this treatment, the engine never failed to sputter to life when I turned the key.

Upon arriving in Chicago, one of the first items on my to-do list was to visit Gene Krupa's gravesite in Calumet City. Admittedly, I was expecting to see a big stone monument, perhaps adorned with a statue of Gene in action behind a granite set of drums. I anticipated something grandiose. To my surprise, I found a simple, ground-level marker with Gene's name, date of birth, and date of death engraved on top resting within his family's plot. I was disappointed at first until I realized that this was a further display of the ace drummer's well-known modesty. He wouldn't have wanted his grave marker to outshine those of other members of his family. Comprehending this only caused me to love the man even more.

I was still in high school when Gene Krupa died in 1973. Upon learning of his death, I felt as if I'd lost a member of my family. Listening to his records assisted me greatly in the formation of my own style of drumming. I played utilizing less of a bombastic and more of a light approach to my drumming. I owe this tasteful style of drumming to the profound talents of Gene Krupa, one of my heroes.

The drums I played were Ludwig. During my stint in Chicago, I also visited the Ludwig Drum Company a couple of times. I toured the factory and spent a whole hour chatting with the company's president, William F. Ludwig, Jr.

* * *

Steve was ruthless and became rather crazy drinking shots of whiskey during the gigs. His worst nights happened when we appeared at the other club on Friday and Saturday. He would verbally abuse me on stage.

"Kick that fucking bass drum, moron!" he'd yell at me. "Get with it, asshole!"

Because I was attempting to discipline myself within my craft, I said nothing to Steve about stopping his voracious onstage ravings. However, inside my head I was in such turmoil that I was constantly close to tears.

I felt embarrassment, anger, self-pity, and a helplessness that I'd never experienced before. I was giving my all and it wasn't good enough. To make matters worse, we played this weekend gig until five-thirty in the morning. I recall the dawn actually creeping in during our final set. These gigs were not only physically exhausting, but mentally draining, as well.

Early on I asked Steve for a raise. He gave me an extra twenty-five dollars each week if I would haul the band's equipment from the gig on Rush Street to the weekend club and back in my van. This included all loading and unloading of the instruments and sound system. Early each Sunday morning after literally crawling off the stage, I still had my loading, hauling, and unloading chores to look forward to because Sunday evening we'd, once again, begin our week playing our "house gig" on Rush Street.

Angelo was the owner of the club where we played on Friday and Saturday nights. He was a well-dressed, mafia-type man. Extremely soft-spoken and charismatic, Angelo reminded me of one of the syndicate bosses from the old movies. One weekend night while we were playing there, a man pulled a gun and was threatening someone—or everyone for that matter. I hid in the men's restroom until the danger was over.

The police soon arrived and the situation was quickly under control. When I stepped out of the restroom, I noticed this man, no doubt the perpetrator, being held between two cops. Angelo silently sauntered over to this trio and, quick as a flash, punched the guy in the head with some kind of a fancy move he'd learned from God-knows-where. The man went out like the light of a dropped table lamp. The cops then dragged the man's limp form out of the club. With complete debonair, Angelo straightened his tie and floated back to the bar. Suddenly, it was time for us to get back onstage.

In early spring, after around one hundred days of playing nonstop, forty-six hours weekly, I booked a flight home to visit and relax for a few days. This was my very first experience traveling on a commercial airliner. The less-than-three-hundred-mile journey was brief, but I loved every short minute of it.

Once back in Cedar Rapids, I felt like a hero and really enjoyed this time reuniting with friends and sitting in with bands. This was a blast! All my musician friends received me with open arms. After all, I was the nineteen-year-old big-city drummer!

Upon returning to Chicago after my time off, I informed Steve I was leaving his band and going on the road with another group. Then, I officially gave him my two-week notice.

During my time back home and in Cedar Rapids barhopping, my friend Ernie Walters persuaded me to go on the road with his newly formed band. His offer seemed heavenly compared to the abuse I was taking during my seven-night weekly stint in Chicago. I accepted Ernie's offer.

Before leaving Chicago, I treated myself to two inspiring shows. In May, I saw Frank Sinatra perform at the Sabre Room in Hickory Hills, a Chicago suburb, and Buddy Rich and his band in Lyons, the same suburb my apartment was located in. Sinatra had reappeared in 1973 after his self-imposed retirement. When I saw him in 1976, he wasn't in top form—as he'd later once again become—but he knocked me out nonetheless. It was difficult for me to believe I was in the same room as this legend. I'd always loved his voice and style. Witnessing this living superstar perform was remarkable and something I'll never forget.

Basically, the place where Sinatra appeared could be described as a dinner club with a stage. Therefore, there was an intimacy that was extra special. The night was magic. I can't express it any other way. Even though I wasn't able to actually meet Sinatra, the night was still a dream come to life. In my opinion, by watching and listening to him perform in person, I witnessed a portion of musical history.

Buddy's orchestra was in top form. Like Frank Sinatra, he, too, performed in a dinner club. During Buddy's second set, I was fortunate enough to sit at a table directly in front of the band. I wasn't so lucky in catching his first set, because I was relegated to a table some distance from the bandstand.

When the band took their first break, Buddy came down offstage and meandered around the club, obviously heading for the front door to get to his bus. The tables he needed to circumvent were rather close together. One of the tables he walked around was where I was seated before moving closer to the orchestra. At this time, I could have simply reached out and shaken Buddy's hand or acknowledged him in some way, but I didn't. At the very least, I certainly could have said "hello" to him, but I declined to do so. I simply looked at him and made no attempt at any kind of recognition. He glanced at me as he walked around the table where I sat. By ignoring Buddy, I somehow felt vindicated for his rudeness to me in Rock Island the previous year. Now we were even. Most likely, Buddy could have cared less whether or not I acknowledged him, but at least I felt better by ignoring the famous drummer.

Unfortunately, this show in the spring of 1976 was the last time I ever saw Buddy Rich in person. I still love him, even years after his death in 1987. As far as I'm concerned, he was and always will be the most exciting, most prolific, most mysterious, most cool, most gifted, and most awe-inspiring drummer in the world. When I saw him perform in Rock Island in 1975, on that fateful night when he snapped at me, I filmed a short three-minute silent movie of him on stage during his first set—before my infamous incident with him. That film remains one of my most prized music-related possessions.

* * *

I was with Ernie's band for only a short time before the band broke up. All the glitter Ernie had promised hadn't materialized. We played a hotel and dinner club chain around the Midwest. The clientele were sleepy, ho-hum vagabonds more intent on eating and having a few drinks with friends before retiring to their rooms than dancing or listening to us play music.

During the summer of 1976, my fiancée, Karen Kopp, and I moved to Oakland, California. Danny Aarhus, my friend and former roommate, came up with a scheme that put my previous dream of playing in San Francisco back into motion. Danny planned to go out there, once again, to attempt to find work in a band. He was hopeful that he could hook up with the same members of the band he worked with during his glory days.

Danny asked me to allow him to travel out there initially to find us all a place to live and line something up for our future musical careers. He'd telephone me when this was accomplished. When I finally received his call he gleefully told me he had found us an apartment, and I was to send him my share of the first month's rent—in advance—before I arrived.

42

We loaded up my poor old van, converted about seven hundred dollars into traveler's checks, and headed for California. Everything I owned was in my van. I was certain this was my future. I was sure we were moving for keeps. We arrived on schedule and unscathed despite the van constantly overheating, a blowout at full highway speed midway though our trip—which took all my driving skills to keep us from wrecking, a broken alternator belt that left us stranded along the interstate, and general travel fatigue. I also suffered a torn muscle in my right shoulder earned in the valor and dedication of keeping my van behaving and on the road for over two thousand miles without the luxury of power steering.

Arriving in Oakland, we discovered Danny had found us an old house to rent. The second story of this house had been converted into two apartments. An old man—the landlord—lived downstairs. We moved in. Danny was already living there on his separate end of the upstairs. Our end featured a modest-size living room, a small bedroom, a large kitchen, and a bathroom. It wasn't until we were moved in and a couple of days had gone by that we discovered that this place was infested with cockroaches. It's strange how you don't seem to notice these disasters in life until a couple of cozy days go by. It's sort of a weaning process. You gradually get used to the place, then—wham!! You're witness to instant eye-opening surprises.

Eventually, the kitchen was the worst. At night, each time the lights were turned on, hundreds of these little, ugly home-sweet-home wreckers would run for cover. I freaked out.

As bad as this discovery was, however, it only became worse when I learned Danny had spent my share of the rent I sent him, making it necessary to say farewell to even more of our ever-decreasing supply of traveler's checks. Even with all this, I probably still would have laughed about it someday if Danny had lined me up with a full-time job courtesy of his former band members. But the good life passed me by in California.

The last straw for me happened the day I sauntered over to Danny's end of the apartment house while he was out, to spray bug killer so his roaches wouldn't scurry over to our side. I was unlucky enough to find his dirty dishes in the sink half-covered with cold, clammy water complete with a sprinkling of dead, floating cockroaches bobbing around the silverware, plates, pots, and pans. Totally repulsed, I wasn't exactly sure what action to take. Danny's hot water heater was located in a corner in the kitchen, and I noticed a few of these disgusting critters venturing out from underneath. Like a good exterminator, I sprayed a couple of squirts of liquid six-legged varmint killer up inside the water heater. To my horror, what seemed like millions of cockroaches began to fall out from inside the lining of this unit. They fell dead, dazed, confused, and no doubt angry, all over the floor. These crawling nightmares had built a nest in there, no doubt, because of the warmth. Genuinely horrified, it wasn't long before Karen and I headed back to Iowa. Danny also soon ventured back.

When all was said and done, I still didn't consider this adventure entirely a bust because I drove my old van over the Golden Gate Bridge. Another memory was made. I was, after all, an optimist.

* * *

Throughout the years, I performed with many bands playing both around Iowa and on the road. I lived in Quincy, Illinois, for several months in

1977, playing with a soft-rock trio there. Surprisingly, during 1978, I even toured with an Elvis impersonator, playing drums in his show band.

Karen and I were married three days after Elvis Presley died in August 1977. Definitely a fan of Elvis' early work, I could tell that, vocally, Elvis learned a great deal from Frankie Laine. I always considered Frankie to be a "song stylist." Elvis was also a song stylist.

My interpretation of a song stylist is a singer who utilizes their voice in the way individual emotions allow them to. There is no particular concern for diction or exactness (other than staying on pitch). They simply sing the way they feel—giving a song their unique interpretation. If they're good at what they do, exceptionality springs forth—a distinctive style is born. This individuality not only distinguishes a singer, but also entices a certain type of audience able to relate to the song stylist. The key is to possess talent and the type of inimitability that attracts the largest audience. Frankie Laine and a few others, including Elvis, became successful song stylists.

In my opinion, some of these singers possess this attraction in a large way, while others do not. The singers who aren't as popular are, in most cases, brilliant but tend to appeal to their own cult following. The song stylist is incomparable. It is unfortunate that most of these unique song stylists never become as popular as those who are status quo.

The status quo singer possesses a pleasant voice and is technically accurate, but sings without emotional involvement with the lyrics, and, in many cases, puts forth an effort that is both uninspired and lacking in individuality. The majority of these singers have made many great recordings. Unlike the fans of song stylists, most people are content with enjoying these status quo singers and their songs without added stylistic artistry. Only the wine connoisseur appreciates the finest vintage.

Commercialism and repetition seem to be the ultimate musical winners. This is evident on most radio stations featuring a music format. Even the oldies radio stations play the same songs over and over because they were the hits. They make money. Sadly, most of the rest of the songs these featured artists have recorded are overlooked and never played on the radio. For every artist (or group of artists) whose hit record plays repeatedly on the radio, you can bet they have several other recordings that are fresh, new, and exciting. But these songs are never offered (unless another is also a hit). This is because we are a commercial society and seem to be satisfied with the status quo.

* * *

During the late 1970s, I seriously concentrated on building up my Frankie Laine recording collection. I bought my first large stereo system in 1978, and dubbed the Laine recordings I collected up to this point onto cassette tapes. I discovered great pleasure hearing these musical gems on my new receiver, and this subsequently built up my musical enthusiasm to an even higher plateau. For the first time, I actually heard these recordings with full fidelity. My goal became to locate all the Frankie Laine records I could find and transfer them onto audiocassette. The time had come for me to build my own library of Laine's recorded works.

As much as I possibly could, I sought out old and used record stores and antique shops. I spent hours sifting through the old records. During the late 1970s, an abundance of old 78s could still be located in these stores. Whether filed neatly, or sitting on the floor in boxes, I sorted through as many of these old platters as I could find. I found many of Frankie Laine's early Mercury records this way.

Consequently, I discovered a sound associated with Frankie Laine I hadn't experienced up to this point. This sound, ironically coming from earlier recordings than what I was used to hearing from Frankie, literally blew me away. I happily discovered that Frankie was also a jazz singer.

These records showcased that sound I loved from the 1940s. The production was there in full force. Each recording I heard was actually prepared in the studio to musically depict the story the song was relating. As far as I was concerned, Frankie was the coolest singer there ever was after producing these spinning works of art. His emotion—wow! It rocked me! I delighted in a singer who connected to his listeners and seemingly understood them. I discovered a connection with Frankie's voice. I was hooked!

One of the first Laine 78s I bought was a worn copy of "Now That I Need You" on the Mercury label, recorded in 1949. This recording was so unique in style and different from anything I'd ever heard before. Another was "Ah, But It Happens," which Frankie recorded in 1947. This song is so full of emotion that it still brings tears to my eyes.

* * *

I joined an ace band in 1979. We played around the Cedar Rapids area. I became friends with Don Daugherty, the bass player, who shared my enthusiasm for Frankie Laine. Don, a few years older than I, better remembered Frankie's peak of popularity. Also, Don's older brother had always been a fan of Frankie Laine.

During the winter of 1979-80, I brought ten of my very best musician friends, including three members of my current band, into a local Cedar Rapids recording studio and produced my own album, which I entitled *That Drummer!* The album was meant to be a career showcase for me, something I could use as a demo. I'd wanted to record an album ever since first listening to Gene Krupa and Frankie Laine records. Originally, I planned to use a great local singer I knew to sing four songs on the album. My part was the drumming. However, after this singer's one too many no-shows, Danny Aarhus, who I made sure was a part of my album project, suggested I sing my own songs. "It's your record, Craig; you sing the songs," Danny said.

Danny promised to write a song especially for me to sing on the album. I never considered myself a singer, but I could carry a tune. Upon discussing it within the studio, four songs, including Danny's composition, were considered easy enough for me to tackle. Danny wrote "I Think I'd Rather Be In Love" for me, and I successfully recorded it. I also sang the standards "On Broadway" and "Summertime."

One of Engelbert Humperdinck's most popular recorded songs, "After the Lovin'," was added to the lineup because of an earlier deal I struck with the members of my band. In exchange for their services on my album, the band would record a few promotional demo songs using my studio time. We recorded the band's demo before most of my vocals were prepared for the album. The band's lead singer sang "After the Lovin'" as part of the demo, and someone suggested that I try singing it for my album. Somehow, I was able to pull it off. We simply dropped the lead singer's vocal track, and I sang over the prerecorded music basic track. It worked out and was added to my album.

Without a doubt, the area's best musicians comprised my album, and many people were awestruck when I produced such a formidable group to work on my project. One of the musicians from my album, Terry Lawless, later went on to make a fortune playing music and traveling with many famous singers. Another one of the musicians who recorded for my album, even though his part was never used in the final cut, was Ernie Walters, my first bandleader boss on the road after my Chicago stint. Unfortunately, Ernie went from being a great guitar player to an inmate for life.

During the mid-1980s, the woman Ernie dated became pregnant. The relationship ended shortly after a baby boy was born. The woman moved in with her parents, and they decided to help raise the child. In June of 1985, on an angry rampage, Ernie drove to their home and demanded they hand over the boy. They refused. In desperation, he brandished a gun and ended up killing the woman's father and wounding others. Ernie then seized his son, the kid's mother, and fled along with a woman he had previously abducted and brought to the scene. He was caught and later convicted of, among other things, first-degree murder and two counts of second-degree kidnapping. He received a life sentence for the murder conviction.

* * *

My album was finished and pressed in the spring of 1980. My daughter, Latisha, was born on November 26, 1980. I was a working musician and a father. Life was good. When she was a newborn, Latisha's bassinet mattress was made higher by placing several of my album covers underneath.

CRAIG CRONBAUGH

The lead singer of my current band leased a club so our band could enjoy a full-time gig. Beginning around 1981, we played at this club six nights a week for over a year. This was the most fun I ever experienced playing music. Even though I lived over fifty miles away and had to commute, I still loved it.

Several years prior to my meeting Don Daugherty, he and his cousin, Glenn Goodwin, had their own popular rock and roll band, the American Legend. This band played all over Iowa, even appearing on local television. During the band's heyday, they became friends with Dave Schneider, a local radio disc jockey. Dave later went to work for Cedar Rapids television station KGAN, which was affiliated with WMT, a large-market and popular Iowa radio station.

After Dave heard us play at the club one night, he invited us over to his house for a party. At the party I asked Dave if he thought I could obtain permission to access the WMT studio record library to look for Frankie Laine albums. The station featured an adult contemporary format, and I was certain they had played Frankie Laine material at one time or another.

Soon thereafter, because of Dave's position within the company, I obtained clearance to utilize the record library, and I was also allowed to bring in my turntable and cassette deck to dub any Frankie Laine albums I needed for my collection. Don accompanied me on the day of the scheduled radio station visit, and we had a ball. I greatly increased my collection by dubbing several albums. Don and I listened to each recording through headphones while the dubbing took place. The whole time I spent taping these albums was as exciting to me as Christmas morning is to a child.

I was exposed to Frankie Laine material that I never knew existed. I discovered a masculine energy and emotion in vocal renditions that were truly awe-inspiring. Up until this time, I recognized Frankie was an emotional singer, but I had no idea anyone could exude so much feeling into a song and carry the listener away with the sounds. It was magic to me.

One of the albums I taped while in the radio library was a 1959 album entitled *Frankie Laine, Balladeer.* As I listened, Frankie transported himself into a true storyteller who could sing and use soul-stirring emotion. I never realized that anyone could express themselves within a song the way Frankie did. It was during this radio library dubbing session, while discovering a glimpse of Frankie's vastness in recorded material, that I made myself a promise: *I will venture on a quest to meet this man and shake his hand. I have to do it.* I can't explain it but even though it was going to be a shot in the dark to meet him, I absolutely knew I would succeed.

I acquired several ninety-minute cassette tapes of Frankie Laine recordings from that radio station recording session. Each morning I played selections from these tapes at home while I was having my coffee. These songs inspired me. Frankie's singing made me feel good inside. I began to realize that music, an emotional art, could actually move a person like beautiful poetry, a special book, or a good movie. Frankie Laine, blessed with the special ability to portray a song, hooked me in a big way.

Finding everything Frankie had ever recorded and transferring the songs onto high-quality cassette tapes became my goal. Unfortunately, I hadn't a clue on how to find out exactly what comprised Frankie Laine's discography.

* * *

We played at the nightclub until around 1983. During my time at this club, I played drums on two songs released on a record for a singer/songwriter friend of mine.

The club was eventually taken over by new management, and we were slowly forced to climb out of our warm nest and seek other band jobs outside of the club. Before leaving this club, two of my records were featured on the jukebox—a single from my album featuring both Danny's composition "I Think I'd Rather Be In Love" and the standard "Summertime," with me singing and drumming, and the record I played drums on with my singer/songwriter friend. This was a wonderful feeling. I discovered how great an experience it is to have your musical work made available to the public.

Since the band and club name were the same, we were forced to devise a new identity for our band. We regrouped, adding a new member here and there, eventually climbing to the point where we were playing music seven nights a week.

During the time our band was regrouping, Karen and I separated and eventually divorced in 1984. She and I, still friends, simply drifted apart. The biggest consequence of our divorce was that I wasn't able to spend as much time with Latisha because I played the band jobs at night. I became emotionally distraught. Prior to our divorce, I was with Latisha each day because we lived under the same roof. Now, living on my own, my little girl was not there when I woke up.

Don's cousin, Glenn Goodwin, became lead singer in our band, and with his polished vocals we released a record in 1985, featuring two original songs written for us by a musician friend. During this time, I was living in Cedar Rapids and playing drums in a band every night.

* * *

A radio station I listened to featured popular music of the 1940s, 1950s, and 1960s. The station was broadcast nationally from Chicago and a local Cedar Rapids affiliate station featured it.

I was listening one late summer day in 1985 when the announcer revealed that singer Frankie Laine had undergone quadruple bypass heart surgery in January. The announcer added that if any listener would like to send Frankie a card, Frankie would, indeed, send a reply. Then Frankie's address was provided over the airwaves. I couldn't believe it! My quest was closer to becoming a reality. I now knew Frankie Laine lived in San Diego. Immediately, I sent him a long letter:

Tuesday, September 3, 1985

From a Cedar Rapids, Iowa, musician.

Dear Frankie Laine,

Let me start off by saying that I was very sorry to hear about your recent illness and trust that now you are fine and that this letter finds you and your wife, Nan, both well.

I am not just another one of your average fans. I not only admire your work, but can appreciate it for its art form since I am a musician. I wanted to write to you to tell you that I am putting together tapes of your recorded career as a family heirloom to be handed down to my daughter and through the generations. I truly love your work. You have a way of feeling the lyric of a song and phrasing that equals no other. Your songs have inspired me many times.

I would like to know how many songs that you have recorded to date. (I so far have over 300.) I would also like to know where I can find your songs to complete my collection. (I've paid as much as $25 an album from a Chicago record shop.)

I am thrilled to be able to write to you having gotten your address from Art Hillyer on a subsidiary radio station in my area. I am 29 years old and started listening to you when I was 14. I saw an Ed Sullivan special and saw one of your early performances, and it knocked me out!

I would very much like to meet you and have my picture taken with you to put with my collection. I cannot afford at this time to fly to California, but will find a way if you will permit me the honor to visit. It would mean a lot to me. You have inspired me through your work more than you'll ever know. I will be one more person who will make sure that your music will be around forever. Please write to me personally as soon as you can.

Very sincerely yours,

Your friend,

Craig Cronbaugh

It was tough waiting for a reply. At one point, I actually didn't think Frankie would write back to me. This musical legend must be a recluse by now, I reasoned. With each passing day, I felt it less likely I would receive a reply. I have absolutely no patience. Anyone you ask who knows me will agree that the one thing I don't possess is the tender art of patiently waiting. I don't know why I thought Frankie would or even should send me a return letter right away, but I guess I took it for granted he would. In reality, I didn't know what to think. I'd never written to a star before.

After almost giving up on an expedited reply, something wonderful happened. Seemingly out of the blue, and true to the radio announcer's words, I received a return letter from Frankie:

> *September 26, 1985*
>
> *Dear Craig:*
>
> *Thank you so much for your very interesting letter. It makes me feel great to know there are people out there listening to me who really care.*
>
> *I really don't know how many songs I have recorded— MANY. I'm happy to report that I am feeling fine after my surgery and am singing again and recording. I have just released a single "SAN DIEGO, LOVELY LADY BY THE SEA" and am finishing a jazz album 'FRANKIE LAINE'S . . . PLACE IN TIME.'*
>
> *Will have my secretary write to you about our Society. I'm sure they would be pleased to have a member like yourself. They also have tapes and records that are available only to club members.*

> *Thanks again for writing, and do keep in touch as I*
> *would like very much to hear from you again.*
>
> *Most sincerely,*
>
> *Frankie Laine*

I was overjoyed! I couldn't wait to tell the guys in the band I'd received word from Frankie Laine. They very much enjoyed Frankie and respected his talent. Needless to say, I framed my letter from Frankie.

On the same day I received Frankie's letter, I also obtained one from the FLSOA, the Frankie Laine Society of America. Frankie's personal secretary, Muriel Moore, wrote me a letter stating that Frankie had informed her about me, and together they were extending me an invitation to join the society. I joined so fast it would have made a figure skater's head spin. Surely this membership would help me to realize my quest: *I want to meet Frankie Laine and shake his hand.*

Since first hearing Frankie sing, I've felt a special bond to him. As a musician, I realize that music is an emotional art. Music isn't worthy unless it's performed with sincere emotion. Frankie feels the song. If he sings a sad song, you can almost hear him cry. If he sings an up-tempo song, you can feel his joy. That's Frankie Laine to me.

Frankie's early presentations of the song "Lord, You Gave Me a Mountain" provides an excellent example of his capacity to emotionally portray a song. Midway through each performance of this 1968 Marty Robbins composition, the tears would begin to stream down Frankie's face and his voice would slightly quiver. The same was true several years later whenever Frankie performed the John Moffat composition "She Never Could Dance." Emotional demonstrations such as these create powerful and unforgettable performances. This caliber of performing is extremely rare among other male singers. Frankie senses each lyric line, interprets its meaning, and projects that interpretation, thus allowing those who watch and listen to experience it.

I felt such an emotional bond with Frankie that I was certain that I would cry at the very moment of meeting him.

Shortly upon becoming a society member, I became pen pals with the society's president, Jerry Massengill. We exchanged letters and even a few phone calls. I was excited to be personally associated with Frankie Laine's society. Jerry seemed glad that I was a member. I was, to put it mildly, delighted when Jerry sent me a cassette tape copy of a very rare recording of two songs Frankie had recorded several years earlier, never before released. Jerry informed me that I was one of only three people in the world to own a copy of these songs. In return, I sent Jerry the album *That's My Desire,* from the 1950s. Jerry had sought this album unsuccessfully for many years. Both of us were very happy with our exchanges. I notified Jerry of my intentions to venture to California and meet Frankie and shake his hand. Jerry readily agreed that I should. I was pleased with what I hoped would be a lasting friendship with Jerry.

I also became pen pals with the society's formally unrecognized vice president, Helen Snow. At this time Helen's name did not appear on the FLSOA stationery. Helen and I wrote to each other, and she became my Frankie Laine collection mentor. Helen lived in Lindenhurst, New York, and came complete with a thick, native New York accent. I enjoyed talking to her on the telephone. She was both informative and opinionated. When Helen was on the telephone line, I knew I was hooked for at least thirty minutes. I enjoyed her letters, as well. I really felt like I was a true member of the *Frankie Laine circle,* thanks to Helen.

Helen's first letter came to me unexpectedly. The letter was postmarked October 19, 1985:

> *Dear Craig:*
>
> *Muriel had given me your name and address. She said you were interested in obtaining some of Frank's old Mercury and Columbia albums. Let me know what you need. I might have extras. I go very often to record meets, and if I don't have what you need, I could get them at the next meet on November 24th. I usually have about four or five extra albums of most of Frank's records. . . . Send me a list and I'll see what I can do.*
>
> *Sincerely,*
>
> *Helen*

I felt like one of the members of the team. I was overjoyed with the discovery of finding a connection to Frankie's material. I always felt that it would be fun to find someone to exchange Frankie Laine stuff with. Helen not only made this a reality, but I treasured it even more because she always looked upon our trades as serious business.

I soon contemplated building my Laine collection in earnest. I began referring to my Frankie Laine endeavors as my *Frankie Laine avocation.* I still regard my associations, collections, and Frankie Laine work as my avocation. After all, it is difficult work collecting Frankie Laine material. Had I collected Bing Crosby, Elvis Presley, or Frank Sinatra, a simple visit to my local record or video store is all that would have been required in order to build my collection. This was not so with Frankie Laine. In 1985, the most I could hope to find would be a "Greatest Hits" album pushed back into some remote corner in a record store, labeled in some generic locale such as the "pop artist" section.

Helen was beginning to make my collecting venture both fun and rewarding. By knowing such a prominent figure close to Frankie, I felt part of Frankie Laine's professional life. During telephone conversations with Helen, she'd explain to me what was going on in Frankie's career, and the phone was always glued to my ear as she related her latest conversation with Frankie. I was *in like Flynn!*

November was the month I embarked upon my quest to meet Frankie Laine. I actually went about coordinating my trip to meet Frankie backwards. I decided when I would go, lined up a substitute drummer for that period, and even purchased a round-trip bus ticket to San Diego—all before even knowing whether or not Frankie could see me during that time.

I telephoned Frankie's secretary, Muriel Moore, from a car-accessible pay telephone early one night on my way to a gig. I asked her if I could meet with Frankie on the following week. She somewhat dampened my spirits by saying, "Oh, Craig, I don't think so. Next week is a bad time to come out because Frankie and his wife are in the process of moving into their newly built house."

"All I want to do is see him long enough to shake his hand," I ventured.

"It's really a bad time," Muriel reiterated. "Can you wait a couple of weeks?"

"I already bought a bus ticket," I sheepishly replied.

Much to my amazement, Muriel announced, "Well, you call Frank yourself and ask him if you can come out. Maybe something can be arranged long enough to be able to meet him."

Then she gave me his telephone number. I was shocked. *I have Frankie Laine's phone number!*

"Am I allowed to call him at home?" I asked in amazement.

"Sure, you're a member of the society, aren't you?" Muriel responded.

I thanked her and hung up the receiver. I was too excited to grasp the realization that I might have angered Muriel. I would pay dearly for that oversight later.

While I was at the same pay telephone, I sucked in my breath and drew upon every ounce of courage I had in my body. Once prepared, I dialed Frankie's number. The phone rang. It was a normal enough ring but, to me, it reverberated like it was coming from Mars. My adrenaline-saturated mind rendered a ringing sound that seemed somehow different. After all, I was calling the home of the great Frankie Laine. There is no way on God's earth Frankie's telephone would ring and sound normal—this wasn't a normal call; Frankie was an extraordinary man.

"Hello."

It was a woman's voice. Then realization hit me that this was Nan, Frankie's wife. Nan Grey, a former movie actress, married Frankie in 1950.

"Hello, is this Nan?" I asked.

"Yes, it is," she rejoined.

"I'm from Iowa and a member of the Frankie Laine Society of America," I rattled. "I'm calling to ask permission to come out to San Diego next week and shake hands with Frankie. That's all I want to do— simply shake his hand."

"Oh, just a minute," Nan replied.

I could hear muffled voices in the background. All of a sudden, a masculine tone came over the line. "Hello."

I'm sure my heart stopped for a moment.

"Is this Frankie Laine?" I asked in a rather hangdog way.

"Yes, it is," he answered.

I disclosed to him what a pleasure it was for me to speak to him. When I mentioned my name, he knew who I was right away.

"Oh, yes, the young man from Iowa," he recalled.

I explained my plans to fulfill my quest. I reluctantly informed him that my bus ticket was already purchased for San Diego the following week. He shocked me by replying, "Oh, Craig, you're not coming all the way out here by bus just for that, are you?"

I felt my courage rising.

"Yes, I must meet you. It'll be well worth it to me."

He asked if I might spend a little time and make a vacation out of it, as well. Unfortunately, I only had a few days off and would need to get right back, I told him.

"Okay, when are you coming out?" he asked.

"The trip will take two days and two nights one way. I'll be there on the nineteenth," I answered.

His next sentence put things in motion.

"Give me a call as soon as you arrive in San Diego. I'll make sure that we get together."

CHAPTER THREE
A Quest Realized

"Ready to go?" Frankie asked, after I'd shaken hands with him just inside the doorway of the hotel. He wasn't angry after all. I was, indeed, ready and apologized to Frankie for not being outside as he had instructed. He seemed surprised that I had a couple of suitcases with me and asked me if I had checked out. I told him I would catch my bus back to Iowa later that same afternoon. Then, he grabbed my smaller suitcase and headed back to the stairs while I picked up the rest of my luggage and followed him down the front steps.

A tall barrel-chested man, Frankie possessed a kind, yet ruggedly masculine-looking face. Even though his hair was mostly white, I noticed as he was walking up the steps that it appeared darker within the shadows. Frankie has worn a toupee for many years, adapting it with both the changes in style and the increasingly graying color of his natural hair. He sported an equally white goatee-type close-cropped beard, which complemented his round, cheery face. Upon first seeing him climbing the steps, his mouth appeared to curve downward as his lips were pursed. This is what initially gave me the impression he might be upset. It wasn't long until he flashed that trademark wide Frankie Laine smile, though, and I knew things were going to be fine.

Frankie's car was parked out front. He unlocked the trunk and picked up and loaded both my suitcases. I kept my briefcase with me. The first thing that Frankie said to me—after we drove off—was, "Well, tell me about Craig Cronbaugh." I think he was fascinated that a twenty-nine-year-old would be interested in music from his era. I told him all about myself. He asked if I had any brothers or sisters and wanted to know what they did for a living. He seemed to be genuinely interested in my life.

I was in a daze. Here I was, riding along in Frankie's car—a new Oldsmobile—with Frankie driving. I looked to my left and there the man was! The singer I admired more than anyone else in the world was sitting next to me, and we were having a conversation! It was an unbelievable time for me.

I proceeded with a little fatherly bragging to Frankie about the most important person in my life, my little daughter, Latisha. He wanted to know how old she was.

Frankie also asked about my music career. We talked at length about music in general. I related to Frankie that, in my opinion, the quality of music in our society attained its peak in the late 1950s, sadly witnessing a decline ever since. I was referring to singers, musicians, and even studio sound quality. He surprised me by responding, "Craig, you have to keep an open mind and accept new trends."

We discussed his famous nickname, "Mr. Rhythm," and he appeared to be perfectly delighted with his world-renowned moniker.

"Your nickname should've been 'Mr. Emotion,' as well," I ventured.

He chuckled and replied, "Yeah, but Johnnie Ray already had that."

When our conversation touched upon his recent surgery we somehow started talking about smoking, and Frankie informed me that he had never smoked cigarettes.

"I have an album with a picture of you on the cover holding a lit cigarette," I interjected.

"They put that cigarette in my hand as a prop for the picture," Frankie explained. "Nan smokes, but I never have."

As I pondered what Frankie had said about the album cover depicting him with cigarette in hand, I suddenly understood and it all rang true. It was supposedly macho for a singer to smoke cigarettes during the 1940s and 1950s. Therefore, why not stick a cigarette in the male entertainer's hand as a masculine prop?

Interestingly, Frankie wore a type of glasses I had never seen before. They were regular glasses that included a clipped-on, flip-up frame, which also incorporated clear prescription lenses designed, no doubt, to increase the focal strength of his regular lenses when flipped down. They operated like those unsightly, utterly not cool, flip-up sunglasses all of us four-eyes have to deal with. I'd never seen this version of non-sunglasses eyewear. I knew from reading about Frankie that he was near-sighted, and his fancy eyewear was most likely designed to help him see better while driving.

As we motored along the San Diego streets, I remarked that it was great that he, a famous celebrity, treated me so nice. At that point I described to him my encounter with Buddy Rich at the Rock Island Fieldhouse in 1975, including Buddy's flaming retort.

"That's bullshit!" Frankie blasted. "Without you people, we wouldn't be where we're at. I never forget that."

I was sure glad to hear Frankie say that. His reply was genuine and down-to-earth. It was refreshing. Frankie was measuring up to every standard I always trusted he possessed.

I asked Frankie if he was recognized much these days. "Once in a while," he answered. "I can live a normal life, though. It isn't like that with some others. Sinatra has to go everywhere with a group of bodyguards."

This answer intrigued me. As the years went by, I became of the opinion that this great entertainer was somehow denied the lasting renown that entertainers like Perry Como, Dean Martin, Johnny Mathis, Frank Sinatra, and many others received. Frankie equaled or rivaled the popularity of many of these singers during the late 1940s and throughout the 1950s, but mysteriously retained less prominence during his later career. Sadly, it seemed that other famous entertainers of the 1940s and 1950s currently received more popular acclaim than Frankie Laine.

Frankie asked me if I was hungry and if I liked Japanese food. I told him I had never tried it. "You'll like it!" he exclaimed. Then he drove us to our first stop since our journey had commenced—a Japanese restaurant.

I strode into the restaurant with Frankie. *Frankie and I walking into a restaurant to eat lunch!* I couldn't believe it. I felt like I was somebody important! *This is too good to be true!*

We arrived at a booth and sat down. A waitress brought us water, and Frankie ordered both of us a glass of wine. *I'm having wine with Frankie Laine!*

I didn't know what to order and Frankie sensed this. "You might try the tempura. It's vegetables coated in a light batter and fried. I think you'll like it," he said.

When the waitress returned, that's what I ordered. Frankie selected something that looked, when it arrived, like an ordinary steak.

After ordering our meal, Frankie began the conversation by asking me what my favorite song of his was. I thought for a minute and told him I had many favorites, but if I had to choose one, it would be both his recorded versions of "Give Me a Kiss for Tomorrow." I love Frankie's rendition of that song, and I think the lyrics he sang are fantastic. I also told him how much I admire his recording of "Black Lace," which was recorded in 1950.

Frankie agreed these were good choices. As I had previously inquired in my letter to him, I asked how many songs he had recorded. He once more informed me he didn't know. It wasn't the answer I'd hoped for. Somehow, I needed to find out how many Frankie Laine songs I still required to complete my collection.

We talked further about his heart bypass surgery earlier that year. (He underwent a second heart bypass surgery a few years later.) He totally shocked me by saying he had almost died and asked me never to tell anyone that. (Years later in his autobiography, *That Lucky Old Son,* Frankie related this near death encounter, so I feel it's now okay to mention it here.) He chuckled with glee and enlightened me by proclaiming he was feeling twenty years younger. I believed him because he was as jovial as I'd always expected him to be. He was like a jolly Santa Claus, and from time to time other restaurant patrons who recognized him and started talking to him from across the room interrupted our conversation. Without losing step, he happily answered them, continually returning to our little *tête-à-tête*. What a wonderful experience for me. It was all like a scene from a movie!

Frankie put me in such great spirits that I, too, started feeling quite jolly. Our food arrived, and as Frankie was adjusting the plate of food set before him, I asked the attractive young Japanese waitress if she knew who it was she was serving. She looked befuddled. "The great singer Frankie Laine!" I chirped. She smiled and nodded as if to imply, *Oh, okay, that's cool. Wait until I tell my friends!* In reality, I'm sure she was simply being nice and putting on an act for our benefit. She'd probably never even heard of Frankie Laine before. I sighed and thought, *Hmmm . . . must be the wrong generation.*

As we started to eat, Frankie took up his chopsticks and expertly began to tackle his food with them. Hard as I tried, I couldn't use mine. Clearly, I couldn't seem to get the hang of it. Frankie attempted to show me how to use them properly by adjusting my fingers to the appropriate location on the two wooden contraptions. To my utter embarrassment, I still couldn't control them properly. So much for an Iowa boy, I guess.

"It's okay to use your silverware," Frankie assured me.

That's exactly what I did and at once began to embark upon my first Japanese meal.

Included with both meals was a side dish consisting of strips of sushi rolled up with steamed rice in the center, accompanied by teriyaki sauce.

I'd never eaten raw fish, and I didn't think I could or even should for that matter.

Frankie persuaded me with gusto, "Dip it in the sauce; it tastes like rare beef."

I tried it, and he was right. We were each given a small plate with four rolls of the sushi. Two is all I could manage to eat. The tempura was wonderful.

I asked Frankie who some of his favorite singers were. Maintaining eye contact, he answered me quite seriously at the very same moment I noticed a grain of rice was stuck in his mustache, "I'd have to say Barbra Streisand and probably Kenny Rogers. Kenny's pretty hot right now."

He went on to add Aretha Franklin to his list. "That woman can really sing! She has balls!! Wow!!" (I later acquired a video clip of Frankie singing as a trio with Aretha Franklin and Jack Jones on the 1975 Academy Awards show. Frankie was a guest on the show and also sang the theme from the movie *Blazing Saddles,* which was up for an award for best movie song.)

We discussed other singers from his generation, including Billy Eckstine, who was always one of my favorites. Frankie spoke highly of Eckstine, but described him in his later years as having developed too much of a "warble" in his voice.

Frankie hit me with another great story regarding the time he met Elvis Presley shortly after Elvis began his recording career. According to Frankie, Elvis happened to be at the same restaurant where Frankie was dining and ambled over to Frankie's table to introduce himself.

Frankie recalled, "He came up to me and shook my hand and said 'Mr. Laine, if I only get to be half as famous as you are, I'll be happy.'"

I was mesmerized.

"Wow, look at how big a star he became!" Frankie added.

Frankie was enthusiastic about his new album entitled *Frankie Laine's . . . Place in Time,* released on his own record label, Score Records. Frankie promised to give me a copy before we parted ways that day. Frankie also recently released a single, "San Diego, Lovely Lady By the Sea" with "The Lady Digs Jazz" on the flip side. I ordered these two songs from the FLSOA before I embarked upon my visit with Frankie. The latter was my favorite song of the two, featuring a somewhat unorthodox jazz vocal. I asked Frankie if that song was difficult to sing and he acknowledged that, indeed, it was.

I was really enjoying this personal time with Frankie. Many times I would look at Frankie and think, *I'm sitting directly across from this musical legend and eating!*

After we finished our lunch, I cheerfully disclosed to Frankie that I must take my chopsticks home as a memento of our lunch together. "Here, take mine if you want a souvenir," he offered as he handed them to me. The chopsticks Frankie used that day are still a part of my Frankie Laine collection. We collectors are, indeed, a strange breed!

Frankie paid for our entire meal. I breathed a sigh of relief. I assumed Frankie would pay for mine, but wasn't quite sure. I hated having to rely on him to do this, but I simply had no choice—I was broke. Relief swirled over me when I realized I wouldn't be left behind to wash dishes while Frankie went on his merry way without me.

When the bill arrived, Frankie whipped out a gold status credit card. To me, this was a further reminder that I was in the company of a regal person. Of course, I realize that Frankie is a human being, just like all the rest of us, but I also believe he is one of what I refer to as the *chosen ones*. They are the humans God chooses and places on this earth to entertain the multitudes. I truly believe this is why we have famous movie stars, athletes, musicians, and singers. Seemingly, only a chosen few achieve worldwide stardom, while others as equally talented, or perhaps even more so, cannot. I can't explain it, but I can verify that I felt a certain aura while I was with Frankie that further strengthened my resolve regarding my theory. Frankie Laine is, indeed, someone very special.

As Frankie was paying, he turned to me and asked, "You're not going to leave those sushi rolls, are you? You can take them with you and eat them later."

"Oh, uh . . . yeah, sure," I answered with uncertainty. He nodded and dutifully requested a sack from the waitress.

When she returned to our table, the waitress threw me an understanding smile and quickly sacked them up for me.

Outside the restaurant, just before returning to Frankie's car, I asked him if he would autograph the 78s of some of his song hits that I brought along. I retrieved my briefcase from his car and carefully pulled the fragile records out. He was happy to oblige by signing his name to each record with a special white marker I'd brought just for that purpose. Just as I had asked, he signed them right over the actual grooves of the black portion of the record, and the bright white signatures stood out like the newly painted white lines on a black highway. He signed all five records I brought.

One of the old 78s was a 1945 recording for Atlas Records entitled "S'posin'." I also brought along the new 1985 release, seven-inch record on Frankie's own label of "San Diego, Lovely Lady By the Sea." I wanted to own signed records recorded forty years apart. I eventually placed both of these records in one frame to depict the four-decade period of time between recordings. The other record sides he autographed were "High Noon," "That Lucky Old Sun," and "We'll Be Together Again." All are now in frames and reside in my Frankie Laine collection.

Once more on the streets of San Diego, we headed for a radio station where Frankie was to be interviewed regarding his new album. Frankie assured me I could sit in the studio with him and watch the interview being conducted. We soon arrived and Frankie parked in front of the radio station. As we crawled out of the car, Frankie opened one of the back doors and from a box of albums pulled out two and handed me one. "Here you go, Craig," he offered. I was thrilled to be personally handed a new album release of Frankie Laine *by* Frankie Laine. He was also happy to quickly autograph it for me.

We strolled into the studio together and found ourselves in a hallway where we were greeted by one of the station's hosts. I was delighted when Frankie introduced me as his friend from Iowa by using both my first *and* last name. The radio guy was very nice, but as soon as the introduction was over, he informed Frankie of an emergency that involved the radio program's scheduled host, and unfortunately the interview with Frankie would have to be postponed.

Ironically, the canceled radio interview worked to my advantage. Since we obviously had some extra time on our hands before visiting the St. Vincent de Paul Center later that afternoon, Frankie asked me if I wanted to see his new house.

I was ecstatic! "Yes, that would be great," I answered, trying not to hyperventilate.

"We are three-quarters moved in, and Nan may be at the other house, but maybe you just might yet get to meet her," Frankie informed me.

Since meeting Frankie earlier in the day, I asked him if there was any possible way to be able to meet his beloved Nan. Over the years I'd heard and read so much about her that I wanted very much to meet her. Helen spoke highly of Nan during our phone conversations. Nan was the love of Frankie's life and a very beautiful lady.

"You will probably get a chance to meet her—we'll see," Frankie assured me at that time.

Nan designed the new house. This would be the permanent home of Frankie and Nan. I knew I was privileged to be able to visit.

We soon arrived at the steel gates of Frankie's driveway. The lane to the house was on a steep incline. I looked over and Frankie immediately shifted the Oldsmobile into low gear for the climb. Shortly, we arrived at the front door of the new Laine home.

Frankie ushered me inside. The house was furnished, even though a few boxes were yet unpacked. Nan wasn't there, so Frankie decided to give me the first-class tour of their new pride and joy. He led the way to the kitchen where I marveled at the thick glass tabletop in the center, with copper cooking pans hanging overhead. The stainless-steel refrigerator was restaurant-size.

Frankie continued the tour by taking me upstairs. I noticed at the top of the stairs a huge portrait of a younger Frankie Laine. What a magnificent sight! We went into the master bedroom, and Frankie sat on the bed and said, "Watch this, Craig." He flipped a switch and the full-length curtains magically opened, revealing a large window area offering a fantastic view. The remote-controlled curtains were something I'd never seen before. Frankie loved them. Like a child, he gleefully opened and closed them a couple of times.

I became slightly embarrassed when Frankie showed me both his and Nan's private bathrooms. I will never forget the gold handles on the toilet in Nan's bathroom, as well as the huge bottle of Shalimar perfume on her vanity. I'd never seen perfume in a bottle that large.

Frankie continued the tour by ushering me inside his walk-in closet. There were rows of shoes all neatly lined up under the immaculately hung clothes. I was seeing more clothes than I had ever seen in one closet. Heck, for that matter, I'd never before seen a closet the size of a room!

Once back downstairs, I was overjoyed when Frankie showed me his music room. There was a wall lined with bookshelves that held all of his albums and piles of seven-inch records. Instantly, I felt as if I were in a gold mine and seeing chunks of gold in front of me within my reach. Of course, my desire was not to take, but only to look at, the wondrous sights I beheld.

Unfortunately, because they were still packed away, I didn't get to see Frankie's gold records during this first visit to the Laine home.

I followed Frankie out back onto his patio. There was to be a small pool in the center. It wasn't quite finished and was empty, but I could imagine its eventual splendor. Frankie walked around the fenced side of the patio and asked me to look at the sight he beheld. He spoke the words I heard for the very first time that day, but was to hear him repeat, not only to me years later, but during countless television interviews whenever he spoke about his home: "I'll sell this view for ten million dollars and throw in the house." He was correct. The view was, indeed, worthy of eight figures behind a dollar sign. I saw San Diego below and all the fishing boats in the harbor. I could see Tijuana in the distance from atop the Laine hill.

Still diligently carrying my camera, I asked Frankie if I could take a picture of him standing on his patio with this spectacular view behind him. Happily obliging me, he struck a casual pose. I snapped a picture. *What a picture for my collection! A photo I took of Frankie Laine!*

Again, I was a bit dubious since the camera belonged to my brother and I was, at that time, unaccustomed to using a manual thirty-five millimeter. I mentioned this to Frankie. As soon as I took his picture, Frankie walked toward me and said, "Now you go over there. I'll take a picture of you."

I adjusted the camera settings so Frankie could simply point and shoot. I posed, Frankie snapped the shot, and *presto,* I had two pictures—one I took of Frankie and the other Frankie took of me—for my collection.

Frankie and I went back into the living room. We sat down at his bar, and he asked if I would like a beer. "Sure," I answered, as he placed a cold can of Olympia in front of my smiling face.

As we enjoyed our beers together, we talked again about show business, and he spoke about the neighborhood he lived in. "Bob Crosby lives nearby," he proclaimed.

During the first lull in our chat, Frankie asked me to call the bus depot to make sure I knew the timetable for my trip back to Iowa. I was quite naïve and assumed they had buses leaving for Iowa all throughout the day and evening. Frankie picked up a phone book and looked up the number of the bus depot, and I called.

"The last bus to Iowa left an hour ago," the man on the other end of the line informed me. "There won't be another bus to Iowa until tomorrow morning." *Oh, no! I'm stranded in San Diego with no money and no place to stay!*

Devastation set in as swiftly as a California wildfire. I was having so much fun and totally sure I was dreaming a pleasant dream, when suddenly this bad news raised its ugly head and seemingly jolted me into another dimension.

"What did you find out?" Frankie asked.

I gave Frankie the lowdown on what the man from the depot told me. Almost in tears, I turned to Frankie and wailed, "I don't have enough money to stay in San Diego another night. I'm broke."

Without hesitation, Frankie reached into his pocket and pulled out all the cash he had there—thirty dollars. He handed it over to me without even counting it. He simply said, "Here ya go."

I was astounded for what seemed to me to be the trillionth time that day. With a breathless voice I vowed to Frankie, "I'll pay you back when I get home."

"Don't worry about it," he simply replied.

A short time later, Frankie announced that he was going to take a nap on the couch for a half hour. It was three o'clock. He instructed me to wake him up at three-thirty.

"Don't let me sleep past that time," he added. "You may take pictures of the house, or go into my music room and look through records, or anything you like."

I was overwhelmed that this man fully trusted me. *What a beautiful person.*

I was overjoyed with the expectation of going through Frankie's records. I thanked him and walked out to his car to grab my briefcase. I retrieved a pencil and pad of paper and while out there snapped some pictures of the outer perimeter of Frankie's "mellow mansion." When I quietly stepped back inside, he was fast asleep on the couch. I silently stepped past him and made my way, once again, to his music room.

Carefully, I lifted up a pile of Frankie Laine 45s and started writing down the titles as fast as I could. I knew my time here would be brief, and I wanted to obtain as many titles as I could so I would know what I needed to complete my collection. Briefly, I glanced through the countless Frankie Laine albums, but mainly focused my attention on writing song titles. At one point I paused and reflected: *Here I am alone in Frankie Laine's music room in his home, and Frankie Laine is sound asleep on the couch just a few feet away!*

This incredible day was one of the happiest days I'd ever experienced in my life, second only to the day Latisha was born.

What seemed like only a few minutes later, I heard Frankie arise and walk into the music room where I was writing titles and ardently wishing I knew shorthand. He had awoken himself early. It was not yet time for me to wake him up. I pondered this, deciding it was probably for the best.

Somehow I couldn't envision myself shaking the great Frankie Laine awake while saying, *"Come on, Frankie, time to get up."*

As Frankie passed by me, he smiled and asked, "Are ya havin' fun?"

He paused and thumbed through some of his albums and handed me a copy of his 1956 Columbia album, *Jazz Spectacular*. The songs for this album were actually recorded in 1955, and the album was released in January 1956.

"This is one of my favorite albums. I have several copies. Would you like one?" Frankie asked.

Since I already had that particular album dubbed onto a cassette, I explained to him that I was collecting his recordings on tape and wasn't really interested in the records (because at that time I figured I'd never be able to find all of Frankie's original albums, let alone own them). Here was Frankie Laine handing me one of his most popular albums of all time for my collection, and I turned down his kind offer to give me this gift. Even now when I think about it, I keenly regret not accepting that album from Frankie.

I continued writing down song titles, while Frankie stepped into the bathroom. By this time, I actually had several written down and almost made it through the entire pile of records when he asked me if I was ready to go to his next appointment—a television taping session.

Once again, we were in his car, and as we rode along, I asked Frankie how many movies he appeared in.

"I was in seven movies," he acknowledged.

I wanted to know the titles, and as he rattled them off, I wrote them down on my pad.

"Ask Muriel to get them for you on videotape," he added.

During more than one instance since meeting with Frankie, he'd instructed me to ask his secretary, Muriel, to supply me with various items. When Frankie was signing my old Atlas 78 outside the Japanese restaurant, he noticed that my copy had a crack running through it. I didn't particularly care about that because I had the record dubbed onto tape and this record was to be framed anyway, but Frankie apparently thought I should have one without a crack in it. "Let Muriel know you want one; she'll get you a good copy," he advised.

I was thrilled with the revelation that Muriel could get me stuff and at once began to naïvely envision her as the human Frankie Laine memento store. Since that day, I've come to the conclusion that Frankie, rightly so, is completely out of touch with the reality of the society, its members, and its business operations. He certainly didn't need to be bothered with the mundane business of running a fan club at this stage in his career. It was an awareness that was to come my way too late, causing me a year of grief.

We headed for the St. Vincent de Paul Center, where Frankie was meeting with Father Joe Carroll to videotape a television public service announcement to the city's less-fortunate citizens. The PSA was to air during the upcoming Christmas season.

As we made our way toward the center, Frankie turned on the car radio, and as we rode along we listened to a mix of what I would term "light rock" music. We were also engaged in conversation. Suddenly, the group Styx entranced the airwaves with their popular hit, "Babe." Abruptly, Frankie fell silent. Our chatter ceased. We listened as the group's lead vocalist, Dennis DeYoung, sang this enchanting song.

I looked over at Frankie and tears were streaming down his face as he spoke in an emotional tone, "That's wonderful. Just listen to those beautiful lyrics."

I was speechless.

Soon, we arrived at the St. Vincent de Paul Center. We were graciously greeted by Father Carroll, who gave Frankie a big hug as we walked in the door. Again, Frankie introduced me by both my first and last name. This time, however, he gleefully added, "He came all the way out here—over two thousand miles—on a bus to stay slightly over one day! He's a nut!!"

I received a warm greeting from Father Carroll, and then he took Frankie and me around to various areas of the center, enthusiastically showing us various rooms and discussing his programs.

After we were shown around, we entered a room where a video camera crew bustled about setting up for the PSA taping with Frankie. To my surprise, Frankie's conductor, Jimmy Namaro, was also there setting up his electric piano. Frankie informed me that Jimmy was to supply the background melody during the taping.

The director of the video asked Frankie if he knew the words to "Silent Night," which, of course, he did. Because the PSA would air during the Christmas season, and since Frankie was a popular singer, a Christmas song was in vogue.

As soon as Jimmy began tinkling around on his piano, I figured it was safe for me to ask for an autograph for my Frankie Laine collection. Frankie noticed me totter over toward Jimmy and also sauntered over and introduced me to his musical partner, using the same endearing "He's a nut!!" introduction. Jimmy, who was a slight, white-haired man, happily shook my hand. I noticed how small and dainty his hands were. (Frankie told me years later, after Jimmy's death, that one of the things he'll always remember about Jimmy Namaro is that he had the smallest hands of any man he'd ever seen.) Jimmy happily provided me with his autograph.

The videographer was soon ready to proceed with the taping, and it was time for Frankie to begin a short rehearsal for the PSA. I felt honored to be in the same small room where Frankie was actually going to sing. *This must be a dream. This kind of thing would never really happen to me.*

The sole end result of realizing my quest entailed merely shaking hands with Frankie Laine. I sought him out and laid out the groundwork, causing my quest to become a reality. I set up the entire project. I traveled two days and two nights on a bus to get to San Diego. The payoff was supposed to be a brief handshake. Never in my wildest imagination did I ever expect to ride in the same car with Frankie, have lunch with him, visit his home, and now watch him sing from ten feet away!

The PSA director handed Frankie a tan knit sweater. Frankie seemed more than happy to put the sweater on, thus completing his camera-friendly Christmas wardrobe. He was seated on a chair directly in front of the camera. A large cue card with Frankie's brief message written out in longhand was placed in front of, and just underneath, the camera.

The director wanted Frankie to complete the PSA without wearing his glasses. Since Frankie, for the most part, appeared in photos, movies, and on television without glasses, the director reminded Frankie that most people retained a mental picture of Frankie Laine without his spectacles.

He was fine with this, but unfortunately, he couldn't see to read the cue card without optical assistance.

As everyone pondered the problem, Frankie rehearsed his simple rendition of "Silent Night," while Jimmy played the melody on his electric piano. I sat next to Jimmy with my tape recorder in hand, ready to record a single version.

As if by sheer magic, the director came up with a brilliant, yet simple solution to Frankie's four-eye dilemma. Frankie was instructed to hold his glasses while he sang "Silent Night," then casually place them on his face before beginning to speak directly to the camera. This worked beautifully and was extremely effective. He read through his lines and "take one" was ready to begin.

I switched on my tape recorder, and Jimmy played while Frankie sang, then spoke. The timing was not quite right, and Frankie was asked to sing the lyrics at a faster pace. The only problem, necessitating several takes, was making sure the speed of both the song and spoken portion were correct in order to fill the allotted PSA time. I found all this quite fascinating, and there's no doubt in my mind that this experience planted a seed in my brain, which was to sprout years later when I began working on my communications and broadcasting degree.

Soon it was a wrap and Jimmy began packing up and, shortly thereafter, took his leave. My trusty camera was, of course, in tow, and I asked the videographer if he would kindly take a few pictures of Frankie and me. He gladly consented. Frankie was also more than happy to oblige. As luck would have it, the professional video lighting—softened by the photo umbrella—was still in place from the video shoot. Frankie totally surprised me by recalling exactly what I told him earlier that day regarding the operation of my camera and informed my newfound photographer that I borrowed this camera from my brother and wasn't quite sure how to use it.

One of the things I'll never forget about this trip was my first-hand experience with Frankie's remarkable memory. Not only did he recall specific events of that day, but Frankie related stories to me of his past complete with the first and last names of the characters involved.

Several pictures were taken, and Frankie delighted me by placing his arm around my shoulder for some of the shots, giving the grand illusion we were longtime, fast buddies. There's no way on God's green earth I could have been happier!

As we climbed back into the car, I again wielded my tape recorder and asked Frankie a few questions. His answers were enthusiastic, as he drove along. To begin with, I asked if he would say a few words to Latisha, who would be five years old in a few days.

"Hello, Tisha, this is Uncle Frank. I guess I'd have to call myself that now since I got to know your daddy. We've had a marvelous time today. We went to a radio station where we were supposed to do a program but unfortunately they canceled it because of an emergency, but then we have spent most of the afternoon filming a cassette tape for the St. Vincent de Paul Center for Father Joe Carroll at a place called the El Cortez St. Vincent de Paul Center. This is a place where they feed and clothe and teach homeless and down-on-their luck people. And

*we just finished the taping now so I'm taking him back
down to the hotel."*

Next, I asked Frankie if he would say a few words about Helen Snow
for me.

*"Well, Helen has been a fan now for quite some time
and apparently has done an awful lot of good work for us
in the New York area, especially in the Long Island area.
And she has a friend there named Lou Monel who is a disc
jockey on WHLI, I believe it is, . . . [T]his guy has a jazz
program on which he features an awful lot of our records.
And Helen, of course, is directly responsible for most of
the good work that Lou has done for us, . . . [O]f course
I'm ever so grateful, and she's really going to work now
on the new album 'Place in Time.' I hope that you like it
when Craig brings it home to play for you all."*

Two of my favorite albums of Frankie's are *Foreign Affair* and
Reunion in Rhythm under the arrangement and direction of the great
Michel Legrand. I wanted to know what it was like working with Michel
Legrand.

*"Well, in the beginning, Craig, it was very scary
because I knew he was such a fantastic talent, and I had
no idea whether or not my musical endeavors and talents
could measure up to what he was gonna hand me to do.
And of course, it scared the heck out of me when we first
recorded in Paris.*

"But the second recording, which we did, oh, several months later, in Hollywood—almost a year later as a matter of fact, . . . [H]e had just gotten married and came out to our home in Beverly Hills and stayed with us. And we spent a whole month together putting this album, 'Reunion in Rhythm,' together. And that one was a little bit more relaxed than the one we did in Paris because I knew him better, he began to talk English a little more, and he was able to understand, and I was able to understand him better, and it was a much more concerted effort. And, of course, the album, just listening to it you can tell how much our relationship had improved by that time."

I asked Frankie what inspirational song, among all he has recorded, was his favorite.

"Well, I think I'd have to say 'I Believe' would probably be the top, and it was the top for ever so long. Until 1968 when Marty Robbins wrote 'Lord, You Gave Me a Mountain' for me. Slowly, that has come to mean as much to me as 'I Believe.' I'd have to say they are probably my co-favorite inspirational songs now."

I closed the interview by saying, "Well, thanks, Frankie, and thanks for your hospitality today. I'll never ever forget it. I love ya."

"Well, I appreciate your comin' down. Anybody who's crazy enough to ride a bus for forty-eight hours to come down and spend a day and a half has to be a little nuts, which I appreciate."

The interview was still in full force when Frankie pulled his car into a parking space directly in front of the Veterans' YMCA, where I'd stay yet another night. We sat in the car until the interview was finished.

After the interview, I packed my audio equipment into my briefcase, and Frankie opened the car trunk and lifted out my suitcases. He helped me carry them to the area in front of the hotel steps. We put everything down and chatted a bit longer.

"Get a good night's sleep, and call me in the morning just before you get on the bus," Frankie very caringly instructed.

I assured him I would and thanked him again for a wonderful day. "I'll remember today for the rest of my life," I told him.

Again, I thanked him, this time off-tape, for his graciousness and hospitality, and, above all, for the loan of thirty dollars, sparing me from utter destitution. I repeated my vow to him that I would pay him back (which I later did), and once more Frankie simply answered, "Don't worry about it."

I handed Frankie a caricature of him that I earlier photocopied onto a piece of paper, asking him if he would kindly write something about our time together. He went back to use the roof of his car as a desk and wrote:

> *To Craig:*
>
> *Great day together! Sure enjoyed meeting you and spending all this time. Let's do it again real soon in Cedar Rapids.*
>
> *Thanx a bunch—Best luck—Frankie Laine*

I still have that framed piece of paper in my collection.

After writing the note, Frankie began walking back toward where I was standing when the driver of a delivery step van, wanting to pull in and park in Frankie's parking space, began to furiously honk his horn at Frankie. With heated passion, Frankie spun around angrily, shook his fist at the driver, and vehemently bellowed a retort. Not wasting any time, the man in the van immediately roared something back. I watched and heard this loud shouting match, but I couldn't make out the heated words. Frankie, mumbling angrily, suddenly marched to his car, got in, slammed the door shut, and started the engine. As he was maneuvering his car out of the space, I noticed a sign posted that read *Delivery Parking Only*.

As the other driver began sliding into the newly vacated parking space, Frankie was parking his car around the corner. Frankie, now fully composed, climbed out of his car, and, for a second time, ambled toward me—his astounded guest.

It was time for us to part ways, and I bravely grabbed Frankie in an embrace and thanked him again for everything. He returned the hug, and in an emotional tone I murmured, "Frankie, I hope our paths cross again."

"Don't worry, they will," he answered without hesitation.

We said our good-byes. Remaining where I was until he returned to his car, I watched while he drove off. His car rapidly disappeared like snow on a May lilac. He was gone.

I suddenly realized how weary I was from the emotion of the day. I had spent seven hours with the man I admire more than anyone. I still couldn't believe what had transpired. As the night shadows crept in, and as I stood there in front of the YMCA with my luggage around me, I noticed someone approach me. She was young—probably in her teens—and looked very dirty and greasy.

"Would you like some company tonight?" she coyly asked.

I was much too preoccupied with the day's events scampering through my mind to deal with this lass of the night, so I took the easy way out.

"Sure, you wait here while I take my luggage to my room, and I'll be back down," I answered.

I picked up my suitcases, ambled my way up the hotel stairs and through the door, checked myself in, and walked to my room, where I stayed put. I had no intention of going back down to be with that girl. This time I wasn't as naïve as when I was nineteen in the Chicago nightclub.

After settling in, I ventured down the hallway to locate a pay telephone to call home. Luckily, I spotted one several feet from my room.

"Hello," Mom spoke from hundreds of miles away.

"Mom, this is Craig. I'm still in San Diego," I happily informed her. "I wanted to call and tell you that I just spent the whole afternoon with Frankie Laine!"

"Oh, my gosh! You did?" was Mom's excited reply.

For the next few minutes I recounted the events of the day to Mom. During most of this phone call I had tears streaming down my face. I couldn't control my emotions any longer. I had predicted I would probably cry upon meeting Frankie because my emotional bond to this man was so intense. The pleasing shock I felt over and over as the events of the day unfolded in all likelihood stopped me from revealing much of what I was feeling at the time everything was taking place. Talking to Mom, however, provided me with release. After listening to my description of what transpired earlier that day, Mom was overjoyed. She replied she couldn't wait to start telling people that her son spent several hours with famous singing star Frankie Laine.

I hung up the phone and returned to my room. This time I decided to take a full shower. I gathered the items I needed before leaving my room once again. After my hasty shower in the communal men's lavatory, I walked back to my small room, crawled into bed, lit my pipe, and began to read my Sherlock Holmes book.

Before long I felt hungry and, because I had nothing else to eat, I opened the sack containing the two sushi rolls left over from my lunch with Frankie. After one sniff of the fishy odor, I couldn't bring myself to eat them. I tossed them, sack and all, into the garbage and listened to the playback of my interview with Frankie.

The interview was fantastic. It was very clean and clear. Frankie's rendition of "Silent Night" recorded fair. His voice sounded clear, but, since he had not sung into a microphone other than the one directly linked to the video camera, his voice was not quite loud enough for my recording. And, since I sat next to Jimmy Namaro during the taping, it didn't help that Jimmy's electric piano was amplified. Therefore, on the recording, Frankie's voice was too soft, and Jimmy's piano was too loud. I was very content, though, secure in the knowledge that I had recorded a piece of musical history. Thanks to this song and Frankie's willingness to allow me to do the brief interview, the four dollar Maxell cassette tape I brought with me was transported to the status of priceless within about six minutes.

I went back to my reading and thoughts regarding my day with Frankie Laine. Frankie is very special. He reacts emotionally to his surroundings.

No wonder he can interpret a song better than all other singers. During the seven hours I spent with Frankie, I observed a bevy of emotions from him. I saw him happy, jovial, serious, angry, and I witnessed him cry. *Wow! What a great soul this wonderful man has!*

I drifted off to sleep shortly thereafter. I'd be willing to bet there was a smile on my face.

The next morning, I was ready in a flash for my bus trip home. I gathered up my luggage and soon was on the sidewalk making my way to the bus depot. I made sure everything was in order for my trip home, then I called Frankie as he had instructed.

"How'd you sleep?" Frankie inquired.

I replied that since I was very tired, I slept great.

"All set to go, then?" Frankie asked.

I said I was and reaffirmed my desire that our paths would cross again.

"Don't worry, they will," he repeated his assurance from the night before.

I thanked Frankie again for transforming this trip into a memory never to be forgotten. Then we said good-bye.

When I hung up the phone, I pondered his quick conviction that our paths would cross again. I didn't know at the time, but he would be proven correct.

CHAPTER FOUR
We'll Be Together Again

When the bus finally pulled into the depot in Cedar Rapids, I sighed with enormous relief. The journey back to Iowa was miserable. With my shortage of cash I barely could afford to eat anything during our stops along the route. I was hungry, exhausted, and just plain travel-weary. At each bus stop, I carefully hauled my briefcase with me into every restaurant we stopped at for my "hearty" meal of coffee and a doughnut or perhaps an order of toast.

Constantly, I opened my briefcase to look over the precious Frankie Laine signed records, making sure they were surviving the journey. I carefully and lovingly patted my roll of camera film containing my very first and tremendously treasured pictures with Frankie. Gently removing it from its case, I marveled at the gold Maxell label on my cassette tape and thought this appropriate because of the precious golden audio that firmly and permanently adhered to the magnetic tape.

Excitement and adventure made the otherwise less than comfy trip out to California more palatable. The return journey home, however, seemed to take twice as long as the trip out there. I suppose the seemingly additional longevity of this ride home resulted from my desire to get back and share my extraordinary Frankie Laine adventure with family and friends.

Just before I embarked upon my quest to meet Frankie, Jerry Massengill had promised to make me an "Iowa representative" for the FLSOA. He explained that I wasn't authorized to open a chapter, since there was only one official American society, but I could become a representative for my state. I informed Frankie of this during our time together in San Diego, and he became very businesslike, explaining he would have Muriel send me copies of *Frankie Laine's . . . Place in Time,* to distribute to radio stations in Iowa. I felt very important.

I resumed playing music every night of the week. A young gentleman who enjoyed listening to our band had discovered my Frankie Laine adventure. By now, all my friends knew about it, as well as many of the regular followers of our band. This young man was a reporter for the *Marion Sentinel,* a newspaper in Marion, Iowa. We happened to be playing in Marion one evening, and during one of our breaks he approached me, introduced himself, and asked if he could have the exclusive on my Frankie Laine adventure for his newspaper. I couldn't believe it—already I was getting some press regarding my visit. I agreed to be interviewed for an article. I deemed it important for people to realize that anyone can do the seemingly impossible if they believe strongly enough and are willing to commit themselves to develop and place all their energy and focus into their quest. If I could do it, anyone could. Of course, I was lucky enough to not only bring my quest to fruition, but to go beyond my expectations thanks to Frankie's genuine warmth and caring persona.

I thoroughly enjoyed being interviewed. This was the first time I formally related my Frankie Laine adventure. It was fun to relive it. I felt myself glow in the warmth of the Laine hospitality, all over again. The *Sentinel* article hit the newsstands on December 12, 1985, with the well-meaning, but slightly misguided headline: "2,000-Plus-Mile Bus Trip To Visit Idol, Frankie Laine, Was Nothing For Craig!"

For twenty-five cents a copy, my Frankie Laine adventure would unfold before the eyes of readers for the first time.

I began planning a Frankie Laine party at my rented house in Cedar Rapids. All of my signed Frankie Laine records were snug and cozy in frames, as was the note Frankie wrote about our day together and the *Sentinel* article. The pictures of Frankie and me were also lovingly placed in frames. All of these bordered memories found themselves hanging joyously on my Frankie Laine wall.

I assembled my recorded Frankie Laine interview, the taped recordings Jerry sent me of the two unreleased Frankie Laine songs, and other rare and hard-to-find Laine audiotapes to feature at my party. Helen Snow had written earlier, just before my trip to California, and promised to send me a videotape of Frankie singing his hits on a retrospective television show special from 1984. Each day I kept hoping for this tape to arrive. I scheduled it to be a huge highlight of my party. My guests would actually *see* Frankie perform.

In 1985, home video was in its infancy. Generally, the only way to watch a particular performance was if it aired on television. Because of this, I was excited to feature the videotape Helen promised to send.

After I arrived home from my California trip, I sent a letter to Muriel Moore asking if I could purchase Frankie's movies on videotape. This is exactly what Frankie had suggested I do in order to get copies of his movies. I couldn't wait to see Frankie in action during his peak of popularity. My excitement waned when I received a note from Muriel a short time later stating she didn't have copies of Frankie's movies. Apparently, Frankie must have thought she had access to them.

Just prior to my party, I wondered why I hadn't heard from Helen. Not able to wait any longer, I telephoned her regarding the promised videotape. I noticed right away she wasn't her happy-go-lucky, upbeat self. Her voice was subdued, and she spoke to me in a virtual monotone. When I asked about the video she informed me she wouldn't be sending it because something came up. I was disappointed by this strange answer. In order to change the subject, I brought up my recent visit with Frankie, and she said Muriel had told her about it. She suddenly and uncharacteristically shortened our phone conversation. I was flabbergasted after hanging up. I contemplated this sudden lack of communication from Helen.

I hadn't received my certificate to be an Iowa representative for the society from Jerry; Muriel's reply was short and to the point regarding Frankie's movies; and now I wasn't going to receive my video from Helen. *What the hell is going on?*

My party was a success, and all my guests had fun. It was a small gathering, complete with a cake I decorated featuring the FLSOA logo—a line-art outline of a young Frankie in a singing stance. Everyone delighted in the news about my trip and the various mementos and recordings. It was great fun to share this.

Shortly after the evening of my Frankie Laine party, I received a letter from Jerry written on the society's letterhead. I had a foreboding the instant I opened the letter and found the recently submitted check for my society dues tucked inside. I read the letter and almost collapsed. The society revoked my membership! The reasons listed included my refusal to accept Muriel's advice when she recommended I wait to visit Frankie during a more opportune time and my requests for Frankie Laine material from both Muriel and Helen. It stung as I read the lines that reminded me that the society is for the promotion and benefit of Frankie Laine and his music and not for personal or material gain.

After reading the letter, I stood there while total and utter devastation set in. Immediately, I figured Frankie was also angry with me. I couldn't live with that thought! How could I possibly listen to my beloved Laine recordings knowing that Frankie hated me? I almost became physically sick. The worst thoughts I could imagine crept like a hooded creature into my brain. *I am barred!! I am exiled!! I'm no good!! Frankie Laine hates me!! My newfound Frankie Laine friends despise me!! What am I doing? What had I done?! Ah, this is the price I'd pay for my dream-come-true visit with the entertainer I love and feel a special bond with. I blew it—big time!*

I telephoned Jerry. I pleaded and begged him to give me a second chance. He was cordial enough, but resisted my plea to rejoin the society. He reiterated that I disregarded Muriel when she advised me not to visit

Frankie when I did. I explained to Jerry that she allowed me to call and ask Frankie myself. Right or wrong, I had purchased my bus ticket for the trip before my call to Muriel. I informed him that Frankie enjoyed our time together. None of what I said to Jerry mattered. I had apparently infuriated Muriel, Helen, and Jerry, and nothing I could do could change that! I was close to tears begging Jerry to reinstate my membership into the society dedicated to the entertainer I loved. He wouldn't do it. I was in shock when I hung up the receiver.

* * *

We were playing seven nights a week, and I was tired and rapidly burning out. I needed some rest. None of the band members wanted to stop working, though. They feared we would lose our streak of gigs. I guess they were right. Music is a competitive business. Making matters worse, new drunk driving laws in Iowa really damaged the live music business. For the most part, people became reluctant to go out and have fun dancing in nightclubs knowing they might be picked up on their way home and perhaps arrested for consuming too much alcohol. Gigs weren't easy to come by. Musicians considered themselves lucky to be playing—especially full time. Not wanting to run the risk of losing our momentum, the band played on.

Prior to my November visit with Frankie Laine, our band went on a summer tour playing several states including Texas, then out west as far as Wyoming during the summer of 1985.

Mom began having problems with her health. She had heard of President Ronald Reagan's recent health check, which resulted in finding polyps in his large intestine. Quickly, because of the President, colon polyps became a big news item. People were beginning to ask questions regarding symptoms, checkups, and treatments before the polyps could develop into cancer.

When certain symptoms became known, Mom recognized she was experiencing the warning signs of intestinal polyps or tumors. A checkup confirmed she had colon polyps. As fate would have it, medical tests revealed one of her polyps had progressed into a cancerous tumor and required immediate removal.

I spent most of our band tour worrying about Mom and missing Latisha. Early in the tour we visited Graceland, Elvis' home in Memphis, and I also made a vocal recording in Nashville. Despite these highlights, I soon began to abhor the tour because it kept me away from those I loved.

Once our band's road trip was completed, and my family received news that Mom's surgery was successful and the tumor removed, I breathed a sigh of relief. Unfortunately, my relief was temporary.

* * *

While attempting to build my Frankie Laine collection on my own without the benefits of the society, I discovered a film print rental agency specializing in renting old movies. When I sent for their catalog, I was amazed that Frankie's first three movies for Columbia Pictures were listed—*Make Believe Ballroom* (1949), *When You're Smiling* (1950), and *Sunny Side of the Street* (1951). They were expensive to rent, but I purchased the agreement to view them anyway.

I delighted in seeing Frankie on-screen during his youthful heyday. I also enjoyed a lanky young singing actor, Jerome Courtland, who starred in these first three Frankie Laine movies.

Later, from another film rental company, I rented and watched yet another Frankie Laine Columbia movie, *Rainbow 'Round My Shoulder* (1952).

Through my constant vigilance, I located other film rental companies. In time, I found two more of Frankie's movies. It was wonderful watching Frankie on-camera more often in his final two movies for Columbia, *Bring Your Smile Along* (1955) and *He Laughed Last* (1956). These movies also featured a young starlet, Lucy Marlow. I didn't know it then, but both Jerome Courtland and Lucy Marlow would someday cross paths with me.

* * *

I'll never forget 1986. It was the worst year of my life. Mom's cancer manifested its ugly head once again. Apparently, the tumor that was removed had so embedded itself into the intestinal wall that it literally started to consume the lining, which broke through, allowing cancer cells to run rampant outside the confines of the tumor and colon and into her system.

Many times, I was forced to forego a band job, search for a replacement drummer, and drive Mom to the hospital. Dad worked, too, and wasn't always available to take her. She required radiation and subsequently chemotherapy sessions.

Doctors soon discovered another tumor, and Mom was scheduled for more surgery. It was awful witnessing her go through this. In March 1986, just prior to her fiftieth birthday in April, I telephoned her oncologist and spoke with the doctor regarding Mom's outlook.

"I'd say your mom has only a few months to a year to live," she informed me.

I wanted her to pinpoint the timeline for me. "In your opinion, does she have a full year or a few months?" I asked.

"Because of the aggressive nature of your mom's cancer, I would say months," the oncologist remarked.

Those words were horrific. Stunned, I hung up the phone. My mom was dying. *How can I possibly live with this knowledge? Why am I losing Mom?*

I began to drink heavily during my band jobs. I argued with Don Daugherty constantly and, for the most part, ignored the rest of the guys.

My best friend was Rick Boddicker, the keyboard player in our band. He also sang much of the time and played an amplified acoustic guitar. Rick was always there for me. He sympathized in my plight regarding Mom. Rick helped me find substitute drummers for the nights I would be absent. He talked to me about music, trying to take my mind off my dread. It was comforting to have a friend like Rick.

The beginning of the end for me came in June. Our family, in turmoil, was trying our best to cope with Mom's certain demise and making sure she wasn't told her cancer was terminal.

Our band was booked to play a weeklong gig just over one hundred miles south of Cedar Rapids. We drove our band bus, a converted school bus painted black and emblazoned with our logo, thus saving each band member the hassle of driving separately. Rick, who also worked during the day in Cedar Rapids at an audio and video rental business, was forced to commute in his own car each day. I don't know how Rick was able to function on little or no sleep, but he did.

Our lead singer, Glenn Goodwin, hailed from this same area, and his mom lived in a small town close to where we were playing, so we parked our band bus in her yard and slept in the bus after our nightly gigs, thus saving motel expenses.

During the early hours of the morning on June 14, everyone was bedded down in the bus and chatting because it was too hot to sleep. Glenn, who had the privilege of sleeping inside the house, suddenly ambled out to the bus and stepped inside. "Craig, you have a phone call," he said. *Who would be calling me at three in the morning?*

I followed Glenn into the house, and he showed me to the telephone. It was my girlfriend. She informed me that my youngest brother, Scott, had wrecked his van and was in the hospital. I freaked! My girlfriend said she'd make a few calls and get back to me as soon as she had further news. I walked back to the bus in a daze. *What more could possibly happen to our family?*

I sat up talking to the guys on the bus until, a short time later, Glenn returned, informing me that I had another phone call. I ran into the house and picked up the phone:

"Hello." There was silence.

Then, because my girlfriend was crying, she managed to squeak out my name. Frightened, I tried to get her to talk to me and tell me what she found out about my brother's accident when suddenly I heard her younger sister's voice on the line.

"Craig, your brother's dead."

"What?!" I yelled. *I can't believe those words. Scott was only twenty-five years old!*

My girlfriend, now more composed, filled me in on the details. While driving home from a late small-town event, Scott lost control of his van while attempting to go around a curve and veered off the highway. His vehicle hit an embankment and flipped over. Scott was not wearing a seatbelt and was thrown from the vehicle. He died instantly.

I don't know how I made it back to the bus. I told the guys what had happened. I managed to choke out the words, "I need to get back to Cedar Rapids immediately."

We woke up poor, tired Rick. He was the only one asleep during all this. It was Saturday morning and since he had worked the previous day and played all night, Rick was attempting to catch up on his sleep because he didn't have to go back to Cedar Rapids. I quickly apprised Rick of the situation, along with my urgent need to get back home. Since he had the only car there, I asked if he'd drive me back. This bighearted giant of a man didn't hesitate. He shook himself awake, and we jumped into his car. In a flash, we were off.

I didn't speak during the entire journey. I was afraid to. I didn't know if I'd be able to calm myself. Thankfully, and with full understanding, Rick didn't attempt a conversation.

Once in Cedar Rapids, Rick dropped me off at my car. I immediately drove to Urbana. My family was in shambles. It was the most emotional time I ever experienced with them. Focusing on Mom's terminal condition, we were totally unprepared when, seemingly out of the blue, Scott is killed in an auto accident.

Mom was in a trance. She was finished; her bubbly personality was gone, forever. Contrary to Yogi Berra's famous quote, her life was over, *before* it was over. Scott left behind a small son, Shane, and a wife who was pregnant with a daughter he'd never meet.

A couple of years earlier, Scott had developed an abscess on his brain. Suffering from a severe headache, he was rushed to the local hospital. After doctors examined him utilizing a CAT scan, there was no doubt Scott was in urgent, life-threatening danger. He was immediately airlifted to the University of Iowa Hospitals and Clinics in Iowa City. Later, we were notified that Scott was approximately ten minutes from death. The scan showed that Scott's brain was being pushed into his spinal cavity due to the immense pressure from the abscess. The scan saved his life.

Many tense days followed. We thought we would lose Scott. Surgeons removed a piece of his skull the size of a slice of bread in order to clean the infection.

When I first visited Scott in intensive care, I was shocked to see his head so swollen. Scott's head resembled a basketball with eyes. The tubes and devices attached to my brother added to this surrealistic view of a deathly ill young man.

With a weak voice, Scott spoke. One of the things he told me was that he saw Grandpa Cronbaugh, who had recently died. "He was waving at me with a smile on his face," Scott recalled. "As I walked toward him, he stopped waving and motioned for me to go back. This wasn't a dream; it really happened."

I contemplated this: *Was Grandpa trying to tell Scott it was not yet his time to die?*

Miraculously, Scott survived. He lived a whole year without that piece of skull the doctors had removed. It was vital he didn't bump that area of his head because there was no protection for his brain there. A year later, doctors placed a permanent metal plate in the area replacing the bone they removed.

Many times I have pondered why Scott went through this medical emergency, suffered the pain, and endured a long recovery, only to have his life wiped out in an instant on that lonely highway curve a couple of years later. The only answer I can come up with is that a few months before he was killed, Scott and his wife conceived their daughter, Chelsea. I fervently believe this is why Scott survived the brain abscess. If he had died at that time, Chelsea would not exist. I wouldn't have my beloved niece.

During our 1985 summer tour with the band, we played a week at a club in Laramie, Wyoming. During the time we were there, a convention for notable physicists was also being held. One evening, renowned physicist Allan Cormack showed up at the club where we were performing. He was playing pool when I approached him during a break. He was a funny-looking man with black-rimmed glasses. His can of Olympia beer rested stoically on the edge of the pool table.

I asked for, and received, Doctor Cormack's autograph. Proudly, I shook his hand. He was the Nobel Peace Prize winner who co-developed the CAT scan, which was directly responsible for saving Scott's life. I also asked Doctor Cormack if he would kindly sign an autograph for Scott. He was happy to do so.

* * *

Mom died on October 24, 1986. One of the last things she was most proud of concerning me, her oldest son, was my visit with Frankie Laine. She used to brag to everyone about it. Always interested in music and possessing a beautiful singing voice, she never had the confidence to go beyond the confines of her home to possibly explore her talent. She seemed content to live vicariously through me, as she bragged about my musical career and all the stars I'd met. She was proud of my fortitude. She never realized that I was exactly like her—insecure, paranoid, and frightened to go out into the world. I overcame those obstacles by a self-realization that in order to achieve anything in life, I couldn't sit idle and allow the world to go by. I lived by my own motto: *If I do nothing, I'll be nothing.* I emulated my heroes. I listened to music and read books. I became my own favorite story characters. If I was to reflect them, I realized I had to make the effort. Perhaps I didn't achieve lofty goals, but I was experiencing life in a way I otherwise wouldn't have, sitting at home on a couch. Sadly, I believe Mom helped motivate me by providing me with an example of how *not* to live my life.

I loved Mom very much. My outlook on life changed the day she died. The hidden child I possessed within my intellect hid deeper inside me. Life became more serious. An understanding that existence may sometimes be brief, as was the case for both Scott and Mom, gave me a latent courage to dedicate my life to living it as fully as possible.

I held Mom's hand as she took her last breath of life. I watched her as her heart stopped and her skin immediately and methodically turned gray. Upon the instant of death, as she lay motionless with eyes wide open,

I witnessed what I believed to be the whispering departure of her soul, causing her eyes to grow dim much like a weakening battery creates a systematic reduction in a flashlight's glow. A tear trickled down her cheek from her left eye. *Is this her way of saying good-bye?* Perhaps it was a display of sadness since she was leaving us. Maybe it represented joy because she was no longer suffering. My other brother Brad, and my sister Lori, were also in the room when Mom died, as were Dad and Mom's two sisters. Mom would never see her grandchildren, Chelsea Cronbaugh and Justin Beenken, or her great-grandson, Keon Purk.

At Mom's funeral, I played Frankie Laine's recording of "There Must Be a Reason." I dedicated the song to Mom from Dad. Mom was the shining youth of springtime to our family. Now that she was gone, we'd all slowly, but surely, grow old.

The tragedy of losing both my brother and my mom was more bearable knowing I had my beautiful daughter in my life. Reminiscing about my association with Frankie Laine made a tremendous difference, as well. I was close to Frankie each time I listened to his recordings. Frankie's music brought me a sense of viability.

Frankie's singing reflects a portrait of life. His musical interpretation doesn't lend itself simply to the goodness life has to offer, but also to life's realism. Frankie relates a story of life or love in every song he sings. Through his singing talent, he converts stories of life into music, enabling them to become more palatable for us, the listeners.

My Uncle Bob, Mom's kid brother, required a ride to the airport in Des Moines two days after the funeral. He lived in Arkansas. I volunteered to drive him. Ironically, an advertisement appeared in the newspaper proclaiming Frankie Laine was scheduled to perform in Des Moines on the same day I was taking my uncle there. Frankie was touring with his "Frankie Laine and Kay Starr" show and would play the Civic Center on October 29.

My plan was to drop my uncle off at the airport, then stay and experience my first Frankie Laine concert.

After saying good-bye to my uncle at the airport, I drove downtown. I knew nothing about this city. I parked the car and decided to locate all the prestigious hotels in the immediate area surrounding the Civic Center. My goal was to locate Frankie's hotel and possibly meet with him and have a chat. I bought my ticket and moseyed into a hotel and walked up to the desk.

"Is singer Frankie Laine staying here?" I asked.

After checking the guest register, the answer was, "Sorry, no."

I strolled over to a pay telephone, looked up several hotel numbers, and began calling, asking if Frankie was listed as a guest. Of all the hotels, no one had him listed.

One hotel desk person rather rudely declared, "We don't give out information on whether or not a star is staying with us!" Bingo! I knew I'd finally found the hotel I was seeking.

A brilliant scheme quickly came to mind. I'd call this hotel again and ask for Jimmy Namaro, Frankie's conductor. Surely, he would be staying at the same hotel as Frankie. Nobody at this hotel would recognize the name "Jimmy Namaro."

Once again I spoke with the "friendly" hotel desk person.

"Would you connect me with Jimmy Namaro's room, please?" I politely asked.

"One moment," came the reply.

"Hello," the voice answered.

"Is this Jimmy Namaro?" I asked.

"Yes," Jimmy responded.

"You probably don't remember me," I began, "but I'm Craig Cronbaugh, the guy who visited Frankie in San Diego last year. You and I met at the St. Vincent de Paul Center."

"Oh, sure," Jimmy fibbed. "Are you with the news media?"

I wanted to find out if I could possibly meet with Frankie before his show that evening. Jimmy confirmed my theory that Frankie was, indeed, staying at this particular hotel. Jimmy went on to add that Nan and their poodle, Noir, were also traveling with Frankie.

"Would you do me a big favor and ask Frankie if I could speak with him briefly this afternoon?" I implored.

"Sure, I'll relay your message," Jimmy complied. "He walks his dog around four every afternoon; I'll ask him to meet with you in the lobby at that time." I thanked Jimmy and hung up the receiver. *Victory!! Yes!!*

I found the hotel and was waiting in the lobby at four o'clock. Shortly thereafter, I noticed Frankie walking down the hotel stairs with Noir on a leash. When he walked past me, I asked if I could speak with him. "I'll be back shortly after I walk the dog," he bluntly replied. I watched while they disappeared through the door. *Well, maybe he is, indeed, angry with me.* It was hell to live my life knowing everyone in Frankie's circle hated me—including Frankie himself!

Soon Frankie and Noir returned, and Frankie strolled over to where I was standing. We shook hands. I asked him if he remembered me, and he nodded, "Sure, how are you?" I informed him that I planned to attend this evening's show, and he smiled. I broke the news to him that my mom had recently died and that she was only fifty years old. As a reply, he slowly and sadly shook his head.

"I played your recording of 'There Must Be a Reason' during her funeral, in her honor, from my dad," I conveyed.

"That song is appropriate," he replied, his voice hushed.

I related the trouble I was in with the society for coming out to visit him last November.

"You got into trouble for that?" he replied with a raised voice and an incredulous frown on his face.

"I guess they're saying I bothered you," was my meek reply. I felt guilty putting the blame on Jerry, Muriel, and Helen.

"Who said that?" he wanted to know.

"Jerry did," I truthfully answered.

"Well, he's out now anyway, and Helen Snow became the president," Frankie gruffly replied. "Call Muriel and Helen and see if you can get them to let you back in."

Happy in a flash, I felt more relief than I had all during the year. I assured Frankie I would contact Muriel and Helen. Apparently, Helen became the president very late in 1985.

I asked Frankie if I could meet him backstage after the concert, and he assured me I could and we would chat further, then he left.

It never quite happened that way, though. After the concert, Frankie came backstage to sign albums and tapes for fans. I sat patiently and watched until he was finished. Tiredly, he strode toward me, shook hands with me, thanked me for coming to see the show, and abruptly walked away.

Strangely, Frankie didn't seem to me to be the same jubilant man I met almost a year earlier. I understood the pressures of traveling on the road and not being in your happy home, so I empathized. As always, he was polite. I guess upon seeing me again I guilelessly expected him to act as if we were long-lost buddies. I was somewhat disappointed, but happy nonetheless. For almost a year, Frankie never knew about the falling out I'd had with the leaders of the society. *Damn, I spent the better part of a year thinking he hated me.* Life is very strange. I suppose that's what makes it so interesting.

The concert was wonderful. Kay Starr took to the stage first. She is an incredible singer and was in great voice. Frankie's show was the finale. I reveled in watching him perform in person. I enjoyed hearing him sing most of his million-selling hits. Once again, Frankie had brought me out of my personal gloom. I was happy, not sad—with one exception—a poignant couple of minutes occurred when, thinking of both Mom and Scott, I silently shed tears as Frankie sang his famous recorded composition "We'll Be Together Again."

CHAPTER FIVE
My Friend Helen

The stress of losing two members of my family within months of each other, combined with playing seven nights a week and not getting to spend much time with my daughter, ended up being too much for me to handle. In addition, I'd just broken up with my girlfriend. After a disagreement within the band, everything came to a head one night during a band job. I uncharacteristically walked away, leaving my drums onstage, the night only half over. I was finished playing music seven nights a week.

I moved from Cedar Rapids to an old farmhouse close to where Latisha lived with her mom. I started working in a restaurant less than ten miles away. I worked as a grill cook on the graveyard shift from ten at night until six in the morning.

* * *

As Frankie Laine had instructed in Des Moines, I wrote both Muriel Moore and Helen Snow asking for reinstatement into the society. In a letter dated November 14, 1986, almost a year after my bus trip to visit Frankie in San Diego, I received a letter from Helen:

> *Dear Craig,*
>
> *After much consideration, we have decided to reinstate you in the FLSOA. I spoke to Muriel, and we decided to give you another chance.*
>
> *I am so sorry to hear of the deaths in your family.*
>
> *Sorry I hadn't had the chance to thank you for Frank's interview and photos, but with everything changing in the club, I had a lot of work ahead of me to straighten out. I'm happy to hear you saw Frank in Des Moines. I had gone to Florida in March to see him and recently was in Schenectady and Elmira, New York, and in Hershey, Pennsylvania, with him.*
>
> *Take care, Helen*

I was back in the society and wasted no time becoming a person who helped locate, instead of ask for, Frankie Laine material. I was also no longer naïve enough to think that Muriel had all of Frankie's stuff.

Moving on and putting behind what had previously transpired, Helen and I picked up where we left off and continued our letter writing and telephone conversations. I know she felt, as did I, that we shared karma, especially when it concerned Frankie Laine. Helen kept me informed regarding all the behind-the-scenes gossip and activities within Frankie's group of people and associates. Even though we lived hundreds of miles apart, we developed a closeness only friends of Frankie Laine can appreciate.

I researched all aspects of Frankie's career. I frequented the library and searched through magazine archives, and I subscribed to various magazines designed for music collectors.

One day, Helen informed me of a television station that aired reruns of the comedy series *Bachelor Father,* starring John Forsythe. Frankie appeared in a 1961 episode entitled "A Party for Peter." Unfortunately, that particular episode ran once, and both Helen and I made this discovery afterwards.

Upon locating the city where the station was, I telephoned directory assistance and was connected to a station representative. Strangely, after hearing my request to rebroadcast the *Bachelor Father* episode with Frankie as guest, they agreed to do so. I was given the date and time the program would be repeated. *I'll videotape this and really surprise Helen!* The only problem was, I didn't own a videocassette recorder. I decided I'd simply rent one and tape it from my television.

On the day of the program, I was helping my great-uncle, who was confined to a wheelchair, by painting a new access ramp to his house. No problem. I rented a VCR from a furniture store in town, deciding to tape the program from my uncle's television. Unfortunately, in 1988, VCRs were not very user-friendly. I opened the little front door of the recorder deck and what seemed like thousands of tiny pin-like levers confronted me. *How the hell am I going to figure out how to record from the television with this contraption?*

In a short while, I was finally satisfied that my genius ability with electronic devices allowed me to set this unit up. Certainly this modern marvel of the twentieth century would do its part.

My uncle and I watched the half-hour show, enjoying every minute of it. I still couldn't believe I requested this particular showing that thousands of people were now watching. My craftiness pleased me. When the program ended, I rewound the videotape. When I played it back, there was nothing but a snowy picture along with "hiss," its audio companion. *No problem—I simply rewound the tape a little too far. I'll let it play a little. The picture will appear soon. Please appear, picture!! Please!!! Oh, no! That piece-of-shit recorder didn't record any of the show!!*

I was disappointed to near tears. My uncle heard me say a few choice cuss words that I'm certain shocked him. I didn't care! Getting this episode on tape was very important to me. I'd gone through a lot in order to set up a rebroadcast of that episode. I wanted to surprise my friend Helen!

I was almost sick for a few days afterwards—every time I thought about not being able to record the *Bachelor Father* episode when I'd had the chance.

Days later, I received a letter from Helen. To put it mildly, I was astounded. Further proving that our minds were on the same wavelength, as far as our Frankie Laine collections, a portion of her letter stupefied me:

> . . . *[W]hen I had gotten home from work, I put the video recorder on and to my surprise, 'Bachelor Father' had been on and the segment with Frankie was on the tape. Did you get this show yet? I was really thrilled to*

finally get the segment. Please let me know if you want
'Bachelor Father.'

When I later received a copy of the *Bachelor Father* episode from Helen, I still couldn't believe my good fortune. Whenever I "discovered" a new Frankie Laine item, I'd make sure to send a copy to Helen. In turn, she always did the same. We really had fun. It was like a business. It was a true avocation.

Helen's husband, John, was frequently ill during the time Helen and I initially became friends. Between working and taking care of John, Helen still managed to touch base with me and exchange pieces of Frankie Laine gold. John suffered with heart problems and later developed cancer. From what I gathered, Helen and John were extremely close. Helen was very honest and up-front with me regarding John's health. She related every detail of his illnesses to me. In return, I gave her as much reassurance as I could from approximately eleven hundred miles away.

Shortly after sending me the *Bachelor Father* video episode for my collection, Helen informed me she would soon have a surprise for me. She referred to me as being her "good friend." In another letter I was a "one in a million friend." One time I sent her fifteen dollars as payment for something she had sent me. She immediately mailed it back, instructing me to buy something for my little girl with the money.

I surprised Helen by sending her several audiocassette tapes of many old radio shows featuring Frankie as a guest. I purchased them through a library specializing in archiving old radio programs. This agency actually performed a computer search on Frankie. To my amazement, their library featured several shows Frankie guest-starred on. I bought copies of them all. The shows were wonderful and encompassed radio programs such as Bing Crosby's *Philco Radio Time* and Spike Jones' *Spotlight Review.* Also included were many of the United States Armed Forces radio shows that Frankie guest-starred on. In all, these radio programs covered a span of years from the late 1940s to the early 1960s.

When Helen received the copies of the shows I'd sent, she was ecstatic! "When I opened your package and looked inside, I said to John, 'Look what that kid did for me,'" Helen related to me over the phone.

After that, Helen became determined to make tape copies of all the Frankie Laine songs I still required for my collection. She sent me a discography, and all I had to do was write down what I needed. Because of Helen, I virtually completed my Frankie Laine audio collection.

Helen and I wrote or telephoned each other on a constant basis. We had a blast discussing Frankie and his music. Thanks to Helen, I was always eagerly anticipating the latest news regarding Frankie's career.

Besides keeping in touch with Helen, I delighted in making my first overseas telephone call. A.E. "Bert" Boorman, of the FLIAS, the Frankie Laine International Appreciation Society, in England, who assembled a remarkable Frankie Laine discography, had been corresponding with me for a while. Like Helen, Bert assisted me with many audiocassette tapes of rare Frankie Laine material. I was grateful to him. He became a great Frankie Laine music collector friend. Each time we spoke on the phone, I thought, *Wow! I'm actually talking to someone in England from my house in Iowa!*

I was even enthralled with the telephone ringing I heard in the earpiece whenever I called England. Unlike within the United States, the overseas telephone rang in groups of rapid twos: *ring, ring . . . ring, ring . . . ring, ring. . . .*

Once, I shipped Bert several videotapes that were a rare part of my collection. He was to view them and send them back. Unfortunately, it was weeks before he received them. It was close to the Christmas season, and I later found out they had been held up in customs. I was afraid my rare tapes were lost. When Bert finally received them, he viewed them and sent them back immediately, and I received them from him in short order. I learned my lesson. Never send a valuable original of anything—anywhere! I would have done almost anything for Bert, though. He's a super nice guy and warm friend.

Helen and I helped each other build up our respective collections. This was so much fun and extremely interesting. In my opinion, that's the purpose of the FLSOA—fans discussing their favorite singer and sharing coveted rarities such as records, tapes, movies, and various other Frankie Laine career memorabilia. We were having a ball.

Unfortunately, because Helen's husband was sick throughout this time, Helen went from being a retired hairdresser to returning to the workforce as a custodian in a high school in order to receive the medical insurance benefit her husband so desperately needed.

Later, Helen managed to save enough money to attend Frankie's eightieth birthday party in San Diego. Lucky for me she was there because I was able to, for the first time in almost a decade, meet my friend face to face.

Frankie Laine

Frankie Laine

Craig's Music Career

In Chicago—1976

Craig—1978

Craig—1983

Craig's Music Career

In Chicago—1976

That Drummer!—1980

Craig and Frankie Laine in San Diego

First photo with Frankie Laine.
November 20, 1985

November 20, 1985

Frankie, Latisha, Craig, and Frankie's wife, Nan.
Frankie's 80th birthday party.
March 30, 1993

Mexican Fiesta.
March 29, 1998

Craig and Frankie Laine in San Diego

Frankie's 85th birthday party.
Humphrey's Half Moon Inn—March 30, 1998

Visiting Frankie at home.
November 12, 1999

Visiting Frankie at home.
July 17, 2000

Craig and Friends in San Diego

With Frankie's brother,
Phil LoVecchio.
Frankie's 80th birthday party.
March 30, 1993

With Frankie's secretary,
Muriel Moore.
Frankie's 80th birthday party.
March 30, 1993

Craig and Joseph F. Laredo, co-author of
Frankie's autobiography,
That Lucky Old Son.
Frankie's 80th birthday party.
March 30, 1993

With Helen Snow, FLSOA president.
Frankie's 80th birthday party.
March 30, 1993

Craig and Friends in San Diego

With Frankie's executive secretary, Mary-Jo Coombs.
Frankie's 85th birthday party.
March 30, 1998

Craig's friend, Norman Foster, from Dumfries, Scotland.
Frankie's 85th birthday party.
March 30, 1998

With Frankie's wife, Marcia, at the Laine residence.
November 12, 1999

Craig's Frankie Laine Scrapbook

Photo of Frankie by Craig—1998

Frankie's 85th birthday cake.
Mexican Fiesta—March 29, 1998

Frankie's 85th birthday cake.
Mexican Fiesta—March 29, 1998

Craig's Frankie Laine Scrapbook

Craig in Frankie's music room next to the
gold record "Mule Train."
November 12, 1999

Craig standing beside Frankie's
portrait in the Laine home.
November 12, 1999

Craig in Frankie's music room.
July 17, 2000

Marlene and Frankie at the
Laine residence.
July 17, 2000

Frankie Laine Autographs

Frankie Laine Autographs

Frankie Laine Collectibles

Rare original fan club record
(late 1940s).

Original FLSOA
membership card.

Rare Mercury picture records
featuring songs by Frankie Laine (late 1940s).
These were manufactured
by Sav-Way Industries, Incorporated—Detroit.

FLIAS membership card.

Frankie Laine Collectibles

Frankie's first record—1944

Silver medallion from Frankie Laine
commemorating his 85th birthday.

Symphony Laine
champagne,
Frankie and Marcia
Laine's wedding gift to
Craig and Marlene
Cronbaugh.
October 2001

Frankie Laine Movies

Make Believe Ballroom—1949; *When You're Smiling*—1950;
Sunny Side of the Street—1951; *Rainbow 'Round My Shoulder*—1952;
Bring Your Smile Along—1955; *He Laughed Last*—1956;
Meet Me in Las Vegas—1956

Frankie Laine Movies

Lobby card to the Columbia movie
When You're Smiling—1950.
Autographed by Frankie Laine and Jerome Courtland.

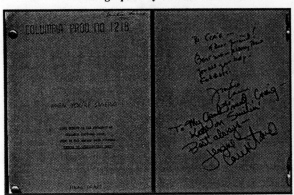

Frankie's script for the Columbia movie
When You're Smiling—1950.
Autographed by Frankie Laine and Jerome Courtland.

Craig with
Jerome Courtland
in Chicago.
October 7, 2000

Frankie Laine Productions

Script cover page signed by Frankie Laine.

Craig during the recording of
The Laine Project.
October 14, 1998

Craig Cronbaugh production, *The Laine Project*, on two CDs—1998.

Frankie Laine Productions

Frankie Laine newspaper articles written by Craig or by other writers regarding Frankie and Craig.

Iowa Public Television taping of *Memory Laine* in May 1999.

Frankie Laine Productions

**Ready to begin Craig's interview by Jimmy Marino for the Frankie Laine documentary.
San Diego—July 17, 2000**

The Frankie Laine documentary
Frankie Laine: An American Dreamer.
JFM International Productions, Incorporated—2003

Frankie Laine Productions

Craig's on-camera scene and screen credit from the Frankie Laine documentary
Frankie Laine: An American Dreamer.
JFM International Productions, Incorporated—2003

CHAPTER SIX
A New Direction

During the late 1980s, I was toiling as a grill cook in a twenty-four-hour restaurant, playing drums with a band on weekends, and experimenting with a radio internship for two hours twice a week.

I enjoyed the radio work. I always wondered what it would be like to work in radio. After all, I was an entertainer in a band so it seemed a natural transition to be on the radio, performing in front of an audience. Many singers, beginning with the likes of such stars as Bing Crosby, became radio personalities without any previous experience, as did many popular musicians. Of course, they didn't have to turn dials, push buttons, flip switches, report the news and weather, and experience the aspect of radio I was learning. These entertainers were strictly radio performers. Even so, I felt it a comfortable transition.

The small station, KGRN in Grinnell, Iowa, featured a soft-rock music format. I spun records, played commercial tape carts, read the news headlines, and even broadcast the latest information regarding missing pets. One of my features included a "fun facts" segment where I fascinated listeners with unusual pieces of trivia. Generally though, I followed the daily programming log. It was fun, but I lacked the necessary voice training required for radio. Grandma Cronbaugh never missed one of my broadcasts. It was great fun to jump in the car after my radio time was finished and travel the few miles to Grandma's house to gain her insight regarding my latest broadcast. She enjoyed listening to me over the airwaves, and then I'd be right there in her kitchen, in person, a half hour later.

I took Latisha to see the radio station one day. She was nine years old. Before we went inside, I asked her not to say anything unless she looked at me first and I gave the "okay." I explained that we might be close to a live, on-air microphone. We went inside, and I introduced Tishie to my boss, also the owner of the station. He turned to her and asked, "How are you, Latisha?"

There was silence. I turned to my daughter, and she was looking at me as if to ask, *"Is it safe to speak?"*

My boss and I both laughed. Latisha had, indeed, paid attention to me by taking my earlier request extremely seriously, not to mention very literally.

Radio is a professional business and requires training and skill to initiate properly. After a few months, I ended my internship.

My current living arrangements necessitated a drive of over fifty miles to my weekend gigs in Cedar Rapids. I was stretching myself too thin working forty-hour weeks in the restaurant and playing on weekends in Cedar Rapids.

My girlfriend and I were back together, but things weren't going well. I soon learned she was having an affair with the guitar player in my band! This was tough on me. I had to play music on stage with our guitarist, who had wronged me. If it is to be performed well, music demands an emotional bond among members of a musical group. A musician must sense this collective awareness of one another on an emotional level. It was almost impossible for me to perform with this guy. I kept things bottled up and simply walked away from him if he came near me. He made matters worse by acting as if nothing had happened. This infuriated me! He tried speaking to me once, and I screamed at him to get away from me, which he promptly did. Mostly, I somehow kept my cool. Playing music in this band was no longer fun, and I performed my drumming chores like a robot. My thoughts were elsewhere. I was a shadow. Nothing was right—everything was wrong.

I moved to a small house close to the restaurant where I worked. I lived by myself and, as always, Latisha would stay with me whenever my schedule permitted. My ex-wife still didn't live too far away. I was grateful that Tish lived fairly close; therefore, I saw her often.

Toward the end of September of 1990, less than two months before Latisha's tenth birthday, I took her with me to Cedar Rapids, where my gig was that evening. The band I was a member of featured a fantastic female singer, Kenda, who was married to the keyboard player, Vic Hernandez. Their daughter, Kyla, is a few years older than Tish. I dropped Tish off at their house to spend the evening with Kyla while we played that night.

Reflecting my unsettled state of mind, I was very rude to the waitress behind the bar at the club we were playing that night. I told her I was sorry after the manager walked up to me and, with passion, said, "You have no right to be disrespectful to my waitress! You apologize to her, or I'll fire the whole band!"

I was growing more and more restless and unhappy. Every little thing set me off. I needed a rest. Something had to give!

When I finished playing, I picked up Tishie. She was sound asleep in her sleeping bag. I woke her up, and then I transported both girl and sleeping bag into the car. Before leaving the city, we stopped and grabbed a quick sandwich.

After we ate, Latisha asked, "Is it okay if I sleep on the back seat in my sleeping bag?"

"Sure, Punkin," I replied.

She was sound asleep by the time we left the city limits on our way toward home. It was just after two in the morning.

A few miles into our journey, we encountered a highway bridge. As I entered the bridge, going south, another car entered at the same time from the opposite direction. I noticed this car swerving into my lane and back out again several times before coming toward the bridge. I wondered what this driver's problem was. The car immediately straightened upon finally making it onto the bridge. I sighed silently with relief. My respite was short-lived, though. As the other car got closer to me, the driver suddenly lost control and swerved into my lane. Our cars collided almost head-on at approximately sixty miles per hour.

When I saw his car's lights point directly at me, I slammed on my brakes. I realized I couldn't turn to the ditch because of the bridge's cement shoulder. My foot was hard on the brake pedal at the moment of impact.

The collision literally threw my car backwards several feet, spinning it so it now faced east. The combination of the impact and the pressure of pressing down on my brake pedal caused bones in my right leg to crumble and my right heel to crack. The sides of my eyes were cut because my glasses literally exploded from my face during the impact. The wind was knocked out of me due to the force of the steering wheel, which hit my chest during the collision. Undoubtedly, wearing a seatbelt saved my life.

Suddenly, I heard Tish cry. Almost immediately I came to the shocking realization she was with me. For a fleeting moment after the wreck, I forgot she was there. I don't know why. Until I heard her cry, I didn't realize my daughter was with me. Perhaps being in shock had something to do with it. I was immediately afraid she was hurt. As best as I could, I croaked, "Are you all right, Punkin?"

"Yes, I'm okay," Latisha sobbed. She became worried when she saw the blood running from the cuts around my eyes.

"Papa's okay," I tried to reassure her. "I think my leg is broken. I can't move it," I added.

All at once, Tish took charge. The two front car doors were jammed, and I couldn't open them. One of the back doors wouldn't open either. Only one back door was operational, and Tish opened it and got out. She immediately went to work trying to flag down traffic.

I was afraid Tish would get hit by a car and kept telling her to stay with me.

"I've got to flag down someone," she responded.

She did manage to get someone to stop. Someone else slowed down, and I heard them yell out they'd go to the next town and call an ambulance.

Tish asked the person in the car that pulled over if they had a jacket for me. The driver handed her a green lightweight jacket, and Tish covered me the best she could. I was shivering by now. I think it was more because of shock than the chill of the early morning air.

When the ambulance arrived, they cut into the buckled car doors in order to reach me. When they pulled me out, I almost fainted.

I kept repeating, "Where's my daughter? I want her with me in the ambulance. Where is she?"

"I'm here," Tish bravely assured me as they hoisted me into the ambulance.

At the hospital Latisha was examined. She was all right. That's all that mattered to me. Because she was asleep and in the sleeping bag, Tishie avoided injury. During the collision she hit the back of the front seat with such a tremendous force that it bowed inward. Since she was both padded and relaxed, she was not hurt.

I spent two weeks in the hospital. I had fractured both my right tibial plateau and calcaneus (heel). I underwent six hours of surgery to repair my damaged leg. Surgeons inserted four steel pins to hold the breakage in place. (I underwent surgery again in November 1995 to remove two of these pins due to tissue irritation in my leg.)

Doctors also placed an external fixation device, complete with four external pins, onto the side of my leg. This piece of equipment held the internal work in place. It resembled a car shock absorber. These pins were literally screwed into the side of my leg. Several times a day, I had the painful task of changing the wrap on the pins and pushing the skin around the holes away from the pins with a cotton swab dipped in a special solution so the skin wouldn't bond to the pins. My calcaneus was left to heal on its own.

I kept a picture of Frankie Laine and me, taken during my visit with him in 1985, on my hospital room bulletin board. Whenever a nurse asked me about the picture, I related my story.

Mentally, I was unsettled with myself. As far as I was concerned, I had failed as a father. A child unconditionally loves their parents. They have an implicit faith that their parents will protect them from danger. I drove the car, and Tishie trusted me to get her safely home. She might have been seriously injured or even killed. I had to deal with that. Feeling I'd let Tish down, I spoke with a counselor on several occasions while in the hospital.

This was a difficult time for me. Making matters worse, the intravenous Demerol I was taking for my pain caused my body to become dependent on the drug. First the hallucinations came. Latisha used to love it when I related the story of how I watched as a little upright tuxedo-clad mouse wearing a top hat and sporting a cane danced merrily each day on the ceiling vent above my bed.

When I was removed from the Demerol, I experienced severe withdrawal. One night I woke up screaming in pain. I called the nurses every dirty name I could think of. I was literally out of my mind. I knew I didn't mean what I was shouting, but I continued anyway. In my mind I was absolutely certain a nurse was picking up my foot and twisting my leg as I writhed in agony. The pain that followed was unbearable. It seemed so real. As one nurse tried to calm me, I kept yelling insults at her and, through my tears of anguish, pleaded with her to stop twisting my sore leg. As she tried to comfort me she said, "Mr. Cronbaugh, your leg has not been moved; nobody has touched you."

I finally calmed down. I cried as I apologized to the nurses. They were wonderful and took it all in stride. My episode was eerily realistic, yet at the same time, a very surreal experience.

My doctor ordered me not to place any weight on my leg. Restricted to crutches upon my release from the hospital, I was home only a short time when I developed a staph infection from the open wounds around the external pins. Returning to the hospital, doctors unceremoniously placed me on a strict regimen consisting of intravenous antibiotics for two weeks. The worst part of this stay was when the doctor had to drain the infection in my leg using a large syringe with a long needle. The pain was so intense during these sessions that I both screamed and cried.

It was determined that the other driver was at fault and was extremely intoxicated when he drove across the centerline into my path. Because he wore no seatbelt, the guy was thrown from his vehicle and suffered severe head injuries. He almost died. He spent many years recovering.

Before Scott was killed, I sometimes neglected to "buckle up." Scott was thrown out of his vehicle. He wasn't wearing a seatbelt. Since the day Scott died, I have religiously snapped my belt on each time I seat myself in a car—driving or riding. Because of this, I believe Scott indirectly gave me the gift of life. Patrol troopers investigating my accident agreed I wouldn't have survived the crash had I not been wearing my seatbelt.

Shortly after my release from the hospital the second time, two troopers from the Iowa Highway Patrol knocked on my door one night. They had a package for Latisha. Unfortunately, she wasn't staying with me that evening, so they couldn't hand her their surprise directly. It was very sweet of them. The gift was wrapped in the sloppy way a man would wrap it, clearly indicating that the troopers did it themselves. Later, Tishie opened the package, and it was an Iowa Highway Patrol teddy bear. The troopers meant for it to be a token of Latisha's bravery for taking such good care of her daddy the night of the accident. My tears flowed.

The whole healing period after the wreck was a learning process. I realized people cared enough about me to go the extra mile. Doctors, nurses, and visitors alike enabled me to get through the worst pain in my life. All these people were there for me. Their concern was genuine, their support invaluable. I'd lost faith in people before the accident. Now it was restored.

It was time for me to begin in a new direction. I was no longer able to work in the restaurant because, even after fully recovering, I couldn't be on my feet for forty hours each week. The night of the accident also marked the end of my music career. Our band played out the bookings we'd had, using a replacement drummer, then broke up. I wasn't going to attempt to get into another band. Maybe one day in the unforeseeable future I'd join a band again; however, for now, those days were over.

As soon as I recovered from the accident, I made plans to attend college. In the fall of 1991, I entered Kirkwood Community College in Cedar Rapids, majoring in Communications Media. My studies specialized in radio and television production, writing, and performance. I attended full time, received good grades, and made the dean's list every semester. Because I was a nontraditional student, I firmly believe I was focused on the tasks at hand and thereby motivated to do my best in college.

As far as I was concerned, I wanted to provide Latisha and me with financial security and adequate health insurance. A career in music wouldn't supply this, unless I was fortunate enough to make it big. That didn't happen. At best, the bands I'd played in were popular in the immediate areas we performed in. I realized I required a career where I could work to achieve goals and live comfortably. Considering myself more mature now with everything that I had experienced within the past few years, it was time to quit acting like a big shot and do something important with my life. Financial aid, two scholarships, a soon to be procured part-time newspaper job, and student loans helped make college a reality for me.

Latisha was proud of Papa attending college. After my first year in college, Tish wrote a letter to Frankie Laine, apparently informing him I was doing well in college. Frankie wrote Tish back on June 12, 1992. Two sentences were dear to me:

> *Glad to hear your dad is doing so well in college. Tell*
> *him to keep it up.*

In my college public speaking class, I chose Frankie as my topic for an informational speech I was required to give. I compiled a videotape of vintage Frankie Laine clips. My friend Rick Boddicker supplied a video projection unit, allowing me to dazzle my classmates with larger-than-life images of Frankie on a big screen. Rick always came through for me. All I had to do was ask and he delivered.

I wrote and gave a complete speech and dressed in a double-breasted suit and tie so I'd represent Frankie's classy style of dress. I admired the way he looked in a suit. His panache was part of his enigma. In the early days, Frankie seemed to favor double-breasted suits. When he sang he moved his arms and hands, but mostly kept his feet together. This art deco v-shaped look endeared him to me all the more. In addition to all of his many attributes, Frankie was a real fashion plate.

* * *

In order to begin honing my journalistic skills, I began writing for a small weekly newspaper in Victor, Iowa, which was close to where I lived. Life kept me busy once again, attending college on a full-time basis and assembling a newspaper, the *Victor Echo,* each week.

Conducting interviews with local area business owners provided a feature under my byline each week. I also wrote a weekly feature story regarding local people of interest. Additionally, I covered all the school board and city government meetings. It was difficult but rewarding work. I wrote my own stories, took my own photographs, and, best of all, was published each week!

My pet goat, Goady, kept me company when I'd sit outside and ponder story ideas. Goady was given to me as a baby by my dad. He was a genuine corker. Goady was neutered, so he didn't possess the unpleasant odor often associated with male goats. His biggest annoyance was women. He absolutely hated them. He liked to butt them with his horns whenever one appeared around my place. Grandma Cronbaugh was particularly wary of Goady. "When he'd come after me I'd grab a switch from the nearest tree and let him have it," she once remarked.

Day after day, Goady proudly strode the yard displaying his gray and white coat. The two parts of his body that he was most proud of were his horns and beard.

Goady's horns were formidable, and because of this, I kept him away from children. He used them mostly to butt both women and cats. I remember one time watching a farm cat eat out of the cat food bowl just outside my front door. As Goady sauntered by, he spotted the feasting cat. This seemed to be too much for Goady, who no doubt figured he should set things right. Gallantly striding over to the cat, he tilted his head down, slid his horns delicately underneath the unsuspecting cat's middle, then, smooth and quick as you please, suddenly whipped up his head, sending the instantly catapulted cat high into the air.

I played games all the time with Goady. During one such game I kicked at his horns, and then he'd cock his head sideways, rear up on his hind legs, and come at me appearing angry. It was all in good fun, and he never hurt me because I knew how to dodge his weapons. But, I suppose he probably would've been just as content maiming or even killing me. That was simply Goady's way.

Goady's beard was a cocklebur magnet. It used to get so full and tangled with those prickly nuisances during the late summer and early fall that his beard eventually became a tightly entwined ball resting snuggly beneath his chin. This mess always took me about an hour to clean, much to Goady's chagrin.

I enjoyed watching Goady's eyes. A goat possesses eyes with a horizontal rectangle-shaped pupil. His constantly moved, depicting his every emotion. I could always tell when he was happy, content, curious, or angry simply by the look in his eyes.

I recall painting a fence one day and hearing a slurping sound behind me. I turned around to find Goady drinking my paint out of the can! He drank it like a thirsty horse at a water trough!

Throughout each day, after eating his fill, Goady chewed his cud, swallowed it, and regurgitated it before continuing chewing. It was fun watching him. Among his favorite snacks, hand soap was at the top of the list. I used to save the little pieces of soap when they'd be too small to use and feed them to him as a special treat. He'd happily chew them up and swallow them. After eating the soap, suds would begin to appear around his mouth!

Goady also ate newspaper and most of my junk mail. One day while I was burning some old newspapers, he grabbed one out of the barrel, which, unbeknownst to him, had just started burning. I tried to grab it out of his mouth. He apparently thought I was attempting to deprive him of his snack so he took off running. Of course, when he ran it fanned the flames up toward his face. The flames ultimately reached his face and caught his facial hair on fire. He didn't have sense enough to let go of the burning newspaper—he just kept running and bawling. It was quite a sight watching a running goat with burning newspaper hanging out of his mouth and his face on fire. Thankfully, he was fine. As soon as the newspaper fire went out, so did Goady's face. He was no worse for the wear.

I had Goady for several years. He was quite a character. When I eventually moved to the city, I gave him to a friend who lived on a farm.

CHAPTER SEVEN
Birthday Bash

When she came over to stay, Latisha always enjoyed listening to Frankie Laine's musical gems with me. I guess she couldn't help it because she had been subjected to Frankie's music ever since she was a baby. As a little girl, Latisha particularly liked listening to Frankie's duets with child singer Jimmy Boyd. Jimmy was the terrific child vocalist who hit big with his rendition of "I Saw Mommy Kissing Santa Claus" in 1952. He and Frankie recorded four duets together during the early 1950s. Tish always asked to hear those particular Frankie Laine recordings before anything else.

As a member of Frankie's society, I was invited to link up with both American associates and members of the international society, to help Frankie and Nan celebrate Frankie's eightieth birthday in San Diego, on March 30, 1993. I hoped Latisha would want to go along with me. I was delighted when she agreed. This would be one more of our great adventures together, before boyfriends and other teenage aspirations demanded her attention.

This was Tish's first time on a plane. I don't particularly enjoy flying. My first flight from Chicago in 1976 was great. For some reason, I've never enjoyed subsequent flights.

I eagerly anticipated Tish's reaction to flying in a plane. She thought it was great. I slept during most of the flight, while Tish, totally at ease, read a book.

Since this was our special time together, I made sure Tish and I did other things while we were in San Diego. We visited the San Diego Zoo one day and SeaWorld the next. It was a blast sitting in our motel room either planning the next day's events or eating tacos from the Jack in the Box around the corner. Best of all, she'd meet Frankie Laine! This time with my daughter was precious to me.

The night of the birthday celebration was wonderful. The party was held in the Marina Ballroom at Humphrey's Half Moon Inn in San Diego. The early spring California sun was shining, and the thrill of Frankie Laine magic was in the air. I could feel and sense the excitement. To top it off, my beautiful daughter was at my side.

There were many people in attendance. Happily, all the friends I'd made through the societies were there. After a lovely meal consisting of Caesar salad, Chicken Marsala, sautéed potatoes, a vegetable medley, a piece of birthday cake, and a champagne toast to Frankie, everyone was free to walk around and chat. Latisha and I were thrilled that our reserved table was directly behind Frankie's table. Frankie and Nan sat there, along with Frankie's stepdaughters and their families.

After everyone finished eating, Latisha moved to the front of Frankie's table and began videotaping, hoping to capture for my Frankie Laine library my anticipated chat with Frankie and Nan. I borrowed a video camera for this event from Rick Boddicker. I waited in a small line to greet Frankie at his table. When my turn came to say hello, I asked Frankie if he remembered me.

"Sure, Craig. How are ya? Good to see you," he answered.

I informed him I had come out to San Diego for his party with my daughter and asked if he'd wave to Tish, who was busy taping. He waved at her as he smiled his big, warm Frankie Laine smile. I wished him a great birthday.

"Thanks, Craig," Frankie replied.

After my brief chat with Frankie, I introduced myself to Nan. Frankie leaned over to her and said, "He's the one we put up at the YMCA."

"Oh, yes, nice to meet you," she replied as I shook her hand.

"He came out with his daughter. That's her, filming," Frankie added to Nan as he pointed to Tish.

What a treasure to meet the love of Frankie's life—his beautiful Nan. Over the years, I heard so much about her that my Frankie Laine avocation demanded that I meet her. I was thrilled to finally introduce myself to this beautiful, gracious lady.

I returned to where Tish was taping, and we both strode back over to the line of persons waiting to greet the Laines. When our turn came I introduced Frankie to Latisha, and I asked someone to take our picture with Frankie and Nan. Immediately, Frankie smiled and, in his jovial way, said to Tish, "You're the one who wrote and asked me about my horse."

Latisha, a lover of horses all her young life, had written Frankie a letter inquiring about his horse almost two years prior to this event. Frankie wrote her back:

> *May 13, 1991*
>
> *Dear Latisha:*
>
> *Nice hearing from you. Glad to hear you are getting good grades in school. An education is so important in order for us to get a full enjoyment out of life. I like dogs very much. Nan and I have a little black poodle.*
>
> *I had a beautiful palomino horse some years ago. His name was Cloud, and he won prizes in some show classes.*
>
> *I'm not working too hard these days. The doctors want me to take it easy after my last bypass operation.*
>
> *Take care and have a nice summer vacation.*
>
> *Cordially,*
>
> *Frankie Laine*

Tish and I decided to mingle a bit at the party. She acted as my personal photographer. How wonderful it was to meet my Frankie Laine friends! I gave Helen Snow a big hug. Even though we were meeting for the first time, by now we both felt we knew one another.

Helen was a rather small woman, with blond hair. She was not at all like I pictured her. I always imagined her as resembling Joan Rivers, since her voice and accent were similar to that of the famous comedienne.

I formally introduced myself to Frankie's secretary, Muriel Moore, who was very gracious to me. Of course, she knew the colorful Frankie Laine admirer from Iowa!

Muriel, a tiny, dapper, and grandmotherly-type woman, bestowed greetings happily floating from one person to another. She wasn't the assertive type of lady I expected, and I found it difficult to believe I had caused this kind little lady to be upset with me in 1985.

I also met and chitchatted briefly with Phil LoVecchio, Frankie's only surviving sibling. Frankie's given name is Francesco Paolo LoVecchio. Phil, the youngest of the LoVecchio clan, arrived from his home in Chicago to surprise Frankie at the birthday bash. My long-distance friend Bert Boorman, from England, also spoke with me. It was an unexpected pleasure to meet Joseph Laredo, who co-wrote Frankie's recently released autobiography, *That Lucky Old Son*. This happened to be the book Tish read during the flight to San Diego. She read the paperback, but I also brought along my hardcover version of the book for Frankie to sign. He happily signed it to both Tish and me. It was an added bonus to obtain signatures of both of the authors.

I wished I'd had more time to speak with each of these people at length. It was impossible because of all the excitement and activity.

During the announcements, Helen spoke briefly at the podium. She read a letter of birthday congratulations from Pope John Paul II. This was quite an honor, and I heard Nan say to Frankie, "Oh, baby," as she kissed him on the cheek.

After Helen spoke, Frankie ambled up to the microphone and spoke briefly. He noted the great turnout and remarked, ". . . [I]t's just gotten bigger, and better and better, and it's resulted in this." Then, referring to the crowded room, he waved his hands back and forth. Frankie closed by becoming very serious almost to the point of tears, "I guess by now you know that I don't have to tell you how much I love you all, and I thank you very much."

As the party was winding down, Tish sat at our table, fully utilizing her right as a twelve-year-old to act a little bored while I walked around the room one more time. It was then I met Norman Foster, all the way from Scotland. Norman was a sensation that evening, because he came to the party dressed in his kilt.

Soon thereafter, the crowd sang "For He's a Jolly Good Fellow" as Frankie and Nan left the room. I watched through the doorway as they walked down the outside steps. When they reached the bottom Frankie spun around with a wave of his arms and sang the last line along with the crowd, ". . . which nobody can deny." Then, he turned back toward Nan, and they disappeared around the corner.

Finally, it was time for Tish and me to leave. We had our table menus, a personalized book of matches, and an engraved plastic spoon commemorating the event as souvenirs. More importantly, Tish and I took with us the memories of this wonderful, enchanted night when father and daughter spent time with Frankie Laine and his friends. This memory from the heart was the best keepsake of all.

CHAPTER EIGHT

Frankie's People

On April 7, 1993, the *Victor Echo* featured a story I wrote about the Frankie Laine birthday party in San Diego, entitled "Fans Celebrate With Frankie Laine." It was my very first Frankie Laine production. Many people around my area read the story and commented on it. It was wonderful sharing my story with readers. I mailed a copy to Helen, and in a letter dated April 20, 1993, she wrote:

> *Great article on Frankie, thanks. . . . It was really*
> *great to finally meet you and your charming daughter.*
> *Wish we only had more time to talk. You must be very*
> *proud of Latisha.*

To my consternation, the video we shot at Frankie's party didn't turn out. The party room was not lit brightly enough for the little camera to tape adequately. It was a pity the video camera wasn't able to capture the event, because Tish taped some neat footage. Oh, well, the world kept on turning.

All of Frankie Laine's people received bad news that summer when Frankie's beloved wife, Nan, died on July 25, 1993—her birthday. The news was published as "News Just Received" at the end of the August 1993 FLSOA newsletter. I'm so grateful I met Nan.

This was the same newsletter that related the news that Jimmy Namaro, Frankie's arranger, conductor, and pianist since 1982, was retiring. I was glad I met Jimmy. I always remember sitting next to him as he played his electric piano in 1985, during the videotaping of the Christmas PSA in San Diego.

* * *

I graduated from Kirkwood in 1993 and transferred to the University of Northern Iowa in Cedar Falls to continue with my broadcast studies. Helen Snow and I kept in touch the best we could. I wasn't home a lot. During most of my time at UNI, I stayed with my sister Lori. She lived less than twenty miles from the campus. On weekends, I ventured back home. I continued working at the *Victor Echo,* until my college schedule made it impossible to keep up with my newspaper tasks.

During my final year at UNI, Dan DeBettignies, one of the chief owners of the Marengo Publishing Corporation in Marengo, Iowa, called me on occasion, attempting to persuade me to join their family of weekly newspapers. I remained uncommitted. Most of my college studies centered around radio and television news writing and broadcasting. Even though I was also training in print journalism, I felt I should initially give radio or television a shot after graduation. Undaunted, Dan continued to call me every few weeks. "Have you thought further about joining us after you graduate?" he always asked.

As graduation drew near, I spoke with Rick Boddicker on the telephone one evening. "I can bring professional camera equipment to UNI and make a good video of you receiving your diploma," he said.

"That would be super!" I exclaimed.

He asked me to give him a call a week before I graduated.

One day, in the spring of 1995, I telephoned Lori from campus to let her know I would be running late that evening. She informed me that I needed to call my ex-wife right away. Shortly thereafter, I called Karen. She stunned me by informing me Rick Boddicker had died of a heart attack. *A heart attack?? He was only in his early forties!!*

I couldn't believe it. Rick was my best friend. We were in a couple of bands together over the years, and he even assisted me with two class projects during my college career. I felt a keen loss. I wouldn't chat with my pal again. Never would we laugh at recalled old episodes of *The Three Stooges*. Gone forever was our sharing of Beatles trivia. I'd in no way forget his generosity or fail to remember how Rick came to my rescue by driving me home, even though tired from lack of sleep, that terrible early morning my brother was killed.

Latisha accompanied me to Rick's funeral. During the fellowship luncheon after the services, Tish didn't want me to leave until I'd said something to Don Daugherty. Don and I hadn't spoken in almost nine years—ever since the night I left the band after a full-blown major battle. I refused to speak to him and started to walk toward the door, but Tish grabbed my arm and pulled me back. "How would you feel if something awful happened to Don like it did with Rick and you never saw him again?"

Tish asked me. She was right. My baby was growing up right before my eyes.

I meandered over to where Don was seated and said, "Latisha won't let me leave until I've said 'hello' to you." That's all it took. Don was his old nice self. We have remained close friends ever since. We wasted almost nine years because of a stupid, unfounded animosity. It took the caring and loving heart of my fourteen-year-old daughter to transform this grudge into a genuine friendship in only a few minutes.

A jam session in memory of Rick took place in Cedar Rapids. Don telephoned me beforehand, asking me to please take part. I was glad to attend. Many of my old musician friends were there. The club was packed. Rick's girlfriend brought a prepared video that was shown to the crowd on a giant overhead screen. It began with our original band demo video from 1985, with me on the drums. There, on the screen, was Rick, larger than life, as if he'd never left us. As it was being shown, I stood next to my table and wept openly. Tish was there also. When she saw my reaction, she walked over and held on to me, giving me strength.

* * *

After graduating in May, I tested the job market waters in the fields of television and radio news broadcasting. It soon became obvious that in order to work in either medium, you must start at the bottom. This meant low wages. Obdurately, I refused to search further. I didn't survive the struggle through four years and two summers of college only to hit the workforce earning minimum wage. The next time Dan called me, I accepted his offer to begin at the Marengo Publishing Corporation. Even though the salary was low to modest, at best, it was well above minimum wage. Besides, I was certain this position would eventually lead to bigger and better things.

The corporation owned seven weekly newspapers and published a magazine for senior citizens. Even though I was immediately assigned writing tasks for the largest newspaper in the corporation, I desperately wanted to also write a human interest feature. I surmised that my Frankie Laine story would appeal to many readers of the senior magazine. I pitched my idea to the magazine editor, Jane Bigbee. Happily, she consented. My writing journey yielded a lengthy narrative describing the first day I met Frankie. It was entitled "My special friend – Frankie Laine" and was published in the August 1995 issue of the *Involvement Magazine*. At the end of the story, I provided contact information through the Marengo Publishing Corporation:

> *If there are any Frankie Laine admirers out there, I*
> *would like to hear from you.*

This garnered a few interesting letters. However, it wasn't until I'd sent the article to Helen that things began happening with the article. Helen wrote, asking if I would allow members of the society to read it. Of course, I was elated!

Helen loved the article.

> *Thanks for everything. You're a great friend. Once*
> *again, I'd like to repeat what a fantastic job you did on*
> *the article.*

I was one of the two members Helen described in the October 1995 FLSOA newsletter:

> *. . . [W]ho have helped to promote Frank . . . . [T]hey*
> *call it a "Labor of Love."*

My name was also published and a brief description of my article appeared. Additionally, the newsletter listed my address for those who wanted to receive a copy. I charged only one dollar to cover the cost of mailing. I received a dozen letters and made another life-long friend— Stephen Fratallone, from California—due to the publishing of this statement in the newsletter.

The same feelings of love and warmth I have for Frankie were replicated time and time again in the stories contained within the letters I received asking for a copy of my article.

A man from Rockaway, New York, became a Frankie Laine fan at an earlier age than me. He wrote:

> *Enjoyed your Frankie Laine article. I'm 56 years old*
> *and have been a fan since I was little. When I finally got to*
> *meet him, his first remark was "Did you like the show?"*
> *He signed his autograph 'Thanks, Frankie Laine.' That*
> *"thanks" describes him well. I thought I was a big fan*
> *and have a great collection of records but you have me*
> *beat. I have four daughters and then a son who is named*
> *after him 'Frank Paul.'*

It was delightful reading an endearing letter from a lady living in Walnut Creek, California. Her letter focused on Frankie's humble nature:

Thank you for sending me your very nice article on Frankie Laine. It was extremely interesting to know how you met him and how cordial and warm an entertainer he is. I really enjoyed the reading on how your friendship grew. It again proves just how "down to earth" Frank really is.

My association with Frank began after his wife, Nan, died. The d.j. of the radio station I was listening to gave his address for anyone who might like to send him a sympathy card. I was so moved by the similarity between Nan and Frank's close relationship and how her death affected him to my own husband and myself. My husband and I had been so close, and he died suddenly of a heart attack while we were on vacation a few years ago. It nearly devastated me, so I sent Frank a sympathy card and a note knowing how he must feel. To my surprise, I heard back from him in a couple of days, and he asked me to keep in touch as he thought he could use my help.

It always both surprised and reassured me each time I noticed the younger generation enjoying Frankie's singing. After all, this was true with my own daughter. Many times I have witnessed what the Laine magic can do to the younger set, and the woman from California reaffirmed this at the end of her letter:

Even my daughter thought he (Frankie Laine) was great. His music will never end. He was always one of my favorite singers.

It was very touching reading the stories of people who love Frankie and his music as much as I do. It's interesting discovering what song began the love affair with Frankie's music and style for someone. One person from Madison, Wisconsin, was partial to Frankie's cowboy songs. He wrote:

> *I just finished reading your amazing story about your adventure with Frankie Laine. I got excited just reading it! Like you, I fell in love with Frankie at a very early age. I was five or six and lived for 'Rawhide.' Every Friday, I was in front of the TV cranking the volume whenever he sang. Drove my folks crazy. I never outgrew that "habit." I still turn him up and let him turn me on. I got my first LP by him when I was eleven. Of course, it was 'Hell Bent for Leather.'*

It seemed that almost everyone who wrote to me asking for a copy of my article had actually met Frankie or had seen him perform at one time or another. The person from Wisconsin stated it very well in their letter:

> *Words can't describe the thrill of meeting such a great man. He is so warm and friendly. I had my picture taken with him and got an autographed LP, too! It was two days after my twenty-first birthday and an event I'll never forget. I'm forty-three now, and I still get goose bumps when I think of that beautiful moment my dreams came true.*

I basked in a warm glow as I poured through letters filled with love for Frankie. Each person put pen to paper, and described their love for this great entertainer. A woman from Memphis, Tennessee, summed it up in a special way in her letter. She wrote:

> *Thanks so much for the copy of your Laine article. Of course, I enjoyed it immensely. Just another example of what a truly special person he is. Can you just imagine such an experience happening with most celebrities?!*

My friendship with Frankie began late in his career. It wasn't until I began to collect videotapes of Frankie's early performances that I realized what a huge star he was while recording for both Mercury and Columbia. Frankie's star shone as brightly as Sinatra's. He was as appealing as Como. He sang as well as Nat "King" Cole. He was as much in demand as any of his show business peers.

While discovering Frankie's vast and powerful fame, it wasn't so much this epiphany as it was the civility of the man that entranced me. I also reveled in knowing that a huge superstar like Frankie was also my friend.

I happily read about the powerful attraction Frankie had on the younger generation during his heyday in a letter penned by a lady from Philadelphia:

> *It's good to share with another admirer how I feel about the man who shared his wonderful talent with us all these years. I'm almost sixty-one years old, Craig, and I went crazy (as young teenagers do) over Frankie from the very first time I heard "That's My Desire." My parents gave me a record player when I graduated from eighth grade (1948), and I proceeded to drive them crazy*

> *with "Mule Train," "Cry of the Wild Goose," "You're All I Want for Christmas," etc., over and over, again and again. There are so many. I think that there is nothing that he recorded that I didn't like. And now that I'm a sixty-one year old "teenager," I still listen over and over, and a day doesn't go by that I don't listen to something of Frankie's.*

I credit myself with possessing a keen judge of character. My initial firsthand experience with Frankie Laine as a person yielded the impression that he was a very emotional being. He couldn't sing and perform the way he does without expressively relating to what he's doing on a daily basis. These thoughts of mine were mirrored in the closing lines of the Philadelphia lady's letter:

> *Besides liking (I should say loving) his music, I greatly admire the man. I feel certain that he is deeply spiritual, compassionate, caring, a regular guy and very decent human being. To me, this makes his music more special and personal. He seems to be truly grateful for his good fortune.*

I was beginning to understand that I was not the only one who had Frankie figured out. A woman from Queens, New York, echoed our feelings in her letter. She wrote:

> *I fell in love with Frankie Laine after the first note—his voice, his interpretations, his emotion, even his breathing. His ability to make me cry, to make me want, to believe in dreams, to believe in man plus*

woman—there's never been anyone who could do that for
me!

A man from Cedar Rapids summed up his feelings succinctly based upon his love of music:

> *I enjoyed your in-depth article about Frankie Laine,*
> *one of my favorite singers from the time when melody*
> *meant something!*

This guy delivered magazines for the U.S. Postal Service. When he received the bundled issues of the *Involvement Magazine* featuring my Frankie Laine article, he noticed Frankie's picture on the cover. That's how he came to read the article.

One member of the FLSOA hailed from Copenhagen, Denmark. He sent his request for my article in early October 1995. He then returned a note with a Christmas card in December:

> *Thank you very much for the copy of the 'Involvement*
> *Magazine' with your story on Frankie. I have enjoyed*
> *very much reading it, and it will stay with my collection*
> *of Frankie's material. I listened to Frankie's music in the*
> *'50s over the radio (AFN), and after a long spell I found*
> *out he was still very active and even singing better than*
> *ever. I hope one day to catch a live performance.*

I arrived home from work one day to find a message on my telephone answering machine from Muriel Moore. On the tape, Muriel mentioned that Helen Snow informed her about my article on Frankie Laine. Muriel asked me if I would please send her a copy so she could read it. Of course, I happily sent Muriel a copy right away.

In virtually every conversation with Helen, inevitably, Tony Cooper's name was mentioned. Tony is the official treasurer and membership secretary for the English FLIAS. He also helps produce both audio and video Frankie Laine productions. Therefore, for many years, Helen was Tony's associate. My inclusion in Helen's conversations about the society in England and Tony's great work made me happy. Helen kept me apprised of every good thing Tony achieved for the English society. I began writing to Tony, and he graciously answered any questions I had. Tony is amazing and, without a doubt, knows more about Frankie Laine than Frankie knows about himself.

The English society has the uncanny ability to locate hard-to-find Frankie Laine career items. The FLIAS members have organized their fellowship into an official entity complete with committee members in charge of certain aspects, such as committee chairman and treasurer. They've appointed a publisher and persons in charge of both the discography and films.

Bert Boorman tirelessly compiled the fantastic Frankie Laine discography, *The Chronicle of a Mercurial Columbian*. I've personally heard Frankie Laine express his gratitude for this discography more than once. By reading through this volume, one becomes immediately aware of the awesome scope of musical material comprising the career of Frankie Laine.

I am continually amazed at the reverence placed upon the subject of Frankie Laine within the English society. Like me, they all regard their Frankie Laine avocations as important. I've often wished I could uncover someone in Iowa who enjoys collecting Frankie's music as much as me.

The British seem to remain loyal to their stars. Unfortunately, this is not necessarily the case in the United States.

I'm proud to be an American. I feel, however, that we Americans don't retain our musical tastes for any long period of time. We change. Change is good, but we don't necessarily continue to covet great entertainers once their commercial value begins to wane. This is possibly the reason why many celebrities who, although very famous in previous years, may currently exist only in shadowy memories.

Unfortunately, in America, Frankie Laine seemed to be one of those forgotten celebrities. I read an article explaining this phenomenon as being brought about because we Americans tend to be what they term a "throwaway society." Perhaps our daily lunches are packed in the types of containers and wrappers that we can simply throw in the trash when we're finished. We may purchase paper towels and other disposable cleaning supplies that we use and toss. We Americans are partial to our everyday items when we need them, but one of the strict requirements that must be met prior to their purchase and use is their ability to allow us to cast them away when we're finished. For the most part, "out of sight, out of mind" seems to be our motto.

Everybody seems to live fast and furious. Manufacturers design products allowing consumers to use and dispose. This use-and-toss feature is becoming a vital prerequisite for many of our products. There doesn't seem to be enough time available in our fast-paced lifestyles to do otherwise.

The bottom line? We are a society that uses and disposes. We even dispose of our stars when we're through with them, leaving only a small number of people to continue to covet these celebrities.

Improvement has been forthcoming concerning these stars. Good old intelligent American enterprise ultimately arrived on the scene. Soon, a door was opened for a possible market directed at loyal collectors.

No doubt this eventually gave birth to the nostalgia craze, which, at first, appealed only to a few during the 1970s. Eventually, more and more people became interested in rediscovering the celebrities of the past, because these stars represent consistent high-quality entertainment. This nostalgia craze helped restore much of Frankie Laine's stardom. His recorded material was being rereleased, repackaged, and was selling again. Frankie, as well as other entertainers of the 1940s and 1950s, began to enjoy a small but notable resurgence in popularity. This, even in a throwaway society.

Thankfully, technology is currently making it possible for a growing number of nostalgia buffs to come forth and purchase almost any item they desire. That's one of the reasons I'm so proud to be an American. Even though it took some time to get started, we are now rapidly becoming a society that caters to every taste.

The British are extremely knowledgeable regarding their cherished celebrities. The FLIAS is a prime example of dedication and knowledge. Whenever I needed a question answered concerning Frankie's career, I simply wrote or called Tony. Because of this, Tony and I soon became long-distance friends, just like Bert Boorman and I had earlier.

Almost immediately, Helen informed Tony about my Frankie Laine article. Tony asked to read the article and possibly recommend its addition to *Laine Lines,* the FLIAS news magazine.

I sent Tony a copy of my article. I was thrilled when he said that it was one of the best articles regarding Frankie he'd ever read. Using his authority within the FLIAS, Tony insisted my article be printed in an upcoming issue of *Laine Lines*. It appeared in number 92, in December 1995.

I was overjoyed to read a couple of responses from members of the English society, published in subsequent *Laine Lines*. For example, in *Laine Lines* number 93, a member from London wrote:

> *I did enjoy the Craig Cronbaugh article in 'Laine Lines' 92. He summed up how we all feel for Frank very well.*

In *Laine Lines* number 94, a British member wrote:

> *Here in the endless fog and freezing misery of the UK in January, this feature was like a mini holiday. I could feel the warmth of the San Diego climate. . . . I looked at the posters for 'Sunny Side of the Street,' etc., and recalled how I saw all the Laine films at my local cinema the first time around before Craig was born. Anyway, a great feature, and we could use more like it.*

Around the same time my article was published, Tony convinced me to join the English society. I became a member in 1995. I've been proud ever since to be a part of such a distinguished Frankie Laine fellowship.

Tony Cooper and I always enjoy discussing Frankie's career. We even have fun agreeing to disagree from time to time.

Thrilled that my article was being read by several Frankie Laine admirers all over the world, I was having the time of my life. It was great connecting with fellow Laine followers. There was one exception, however, that placed a burden on both Helen Snow and me.

I received yet another letter requesting a copy of my article. The letter was from a guy living in Texas. Soon, I discovered he was confined to a wheelchair because of a type of muscle degeneration disease. Tragically, this man had nothing else to do with his life but revere his favorite singers. His was a life of confinement and focus. Apparently, his days centered around extreme wants and apparent needs for celebrity information.

After I mailed a copy of my article to him, he must have felt as though he'd found a soul mate. Because he was a member of the American society, he had Helen's telephone number since it was printed on the front page of each newsletter. He also acquired my phone number after it was published in the issue regarding my article. This poor soul took turns calling Helen and me, keeping us each on the line for long stretches at a time.

Although he was an adult, he lived with his mother, who took care of him. I really felt bad for this man. In the beginning, I very much wanted him to think of me as a friend. I tried my best to be patient with him. It rapidly became quite a task to do so.

A speech impediment, resulting from the disease, caused him to be somewhat difficult to understand, and because of this his telephone calls were seemingly longer. To add insult to injury, his voice possessed a monotone quality, which grated on my nerves. He was also given to attacks of coughing and hacking, which, unfortunately, came often and without warning. When these episodes were over, he'd simply pick up talking where he left off without so much as a word of apology.

He telephoned me sometimes daily or even twice a day! He also bothered Helen this way. Seemingly, no way existed to persuade him to end his constant one-sided speeches peppered with inquiries. He asked questions, coupling each answer with more questions.

"Craig, did Frankie Laine ever record with Rosemary Clooney?"

"No, he never did."

"Why didn't Frankie Laine ever record with Rosemary Clooney?"

"I don't know."

"Why don't you know?"

This went on and on, subject after subject, for unbearable stretches of time. Upon finally becoming satisfied with my series of answers, he moved on with another question on yet another music-oriented topic. To my chagrin, he never gave closure to the answers he received. This was quite annoying. He'd never say something such as *"Oh, how interesting!"* or acknowledge an answer in any way, shape, or form! Only a short pause later, he'd simply ask another question.

Admittedly, the first couple of calls were amusing. He'd actually sing whole songs over the phone. When his calls began interfering with my life, he became too much to bear.

Helen, too, was rapidly becoming weary from all his calls. He'd call her when she'd be running errands for her sick husband, John. Arriving home from work exhausted, she'd often find him on the other end of the ringing phone. Helen became furious when he'd call and bother John with questions when she wasn't at home. After one such episode, Helen royally chewed him out with her hot-tongued vernacular the next time he called. When she was finished with her raving, she abruptly slammed down the receiver, putting an immediate end to the call. Seemingly undaunted by this, and never one prone to giving up, he simply telephoned his old buddy, Craig.

Usually, this guy's standard method was to call back if anyone hung up on him. I tried hanging up on him once. Totally unscathed, he called me back, picking up where he left off, asking away, or singing me a tune.

In due course, I experimented with leaving my phone off the hook. Soon realizing I might be missing other important calls, I abandoned this idea. I didn't know what to do. I required a speedy remedy. My privacy was being invaded!

Realizing what many celebrities must sometimes have to endure provided me with a new respect for the famous. There are some strange people in the world. It's a frightening reality that these celebrity-loving extremists may acquire enough access to disrupt lives. I fully understand the attraction to someone who makes you happy. Without this deep-rooted feeling, I wouldn't have endeavored to make my Frankie Laine quest a reality. Many fans are similar to me in that regard. However, crossing the line can be disruptive to those you seek.

The beginning of the end came when this person who attempted to monopolize my telephone began calling the publishing company I worked for, asking for me. He possessed a knack for finding out information through the various channels available to him. In return for this information, the one lucky enough to be on the other end of the line might be "treated" with his vocal rendition of a golden oldie.

When calling the corporation, he'd ask the receptionist questions about celebrities, keeping her on the line far too long. I'd had it! Taking a firm stand, I warned my musical troublemaker never again to call my place of business.

One day, Helen left a message on my home answering machine. She was almost hysterical, advising me not to have anything to do with this guy. She reiterated what a pest he'd become and instructed me to hang up on him whenever he called. I wondered if she realized that if I did what she asked, he'd probably end up calling her.

Finally, I arrived at a solution. Magically, I convinced this scalawag to telephone me only on a certain date and time—once a month. I think he was becoming aware that I wasn't particularly interested in talking to him so often. By setting up a particular telephone schedule, I persuaded him I would be happy to receive his calls on the given dates and times. Somehow, I convinced him I would not talk to him at any other time. When the date and time arrived for him to call, I simply unplugged my phone. This was a drastic and unfortunate measure, but I really had no choice. It didn't matter that this person had the best of intentions, I just couldn't allow it to continue. I was sad because of his medical condition, but could no longer allow him to control my home life. Eventually, he stopped calling altogether.

The exact opposite occurred when I received a letter from California requesting a copy of my article. The letter arrived from Stephen Fratallone in April 1996. I mailed him a copy right away.

I was excited when he wrote back to me. Not only did he love my article, but he was close to my age and enjoyed my interests in music. Stephen, also a musician, played the saxophone. He enjoyed Frankie Laine's music, and he had also met him. We soon developed into fast friends through the powers of the postal service. Our similar interests were uncanny. Stephen also dabbled in the art of newspaper writing.

Since we were both bachelors and wrote each other so often, we decided to meet. I invited Stephen to visit me for a few days. He thought this was a great idea and began making plans for a trip to Iowa in November 1996.

During the fall of 1995, I was overjoyed when I was given the opportunity to become news editor for one of the corporation's weekly newspapers, the *North English Record*. I was in charge of publishing this newspaper each week.

I was busy with my newspaper work and happily anticipating Stephen's visit when I received sad news. Helen wrote in September 1996, informing me that her husband had died. Her words were heartrending:

> *I'm having quite a time coping with him not being around anymore. I miss him terribly.*

Near the end of her letter she implored:

> *Anyway, please keep in touch when you can. Right now I need all the friends I have to help me make it through this ordeal.*

My heart went out to Helen. I knew what she had endured because of his recent declining health. I vowed to try to be there for her and cheer her up.

When Stephen arrived, we had a blast thoroughly checking out my Frankie Laine collection. Additionally, he assisted me with my newspaper chores. I offered him a writing assignment, and he produced an interesting article regarding the plight of a local cemetery where Civil War veterans were interred. He also took pictures, which were subsequently published, of me giving a speech to a local group organization.

I was selected to be the drummer in an orchestra comprised of area band instructors, "The Directors' Jazz Band," scheduled to perform during an area high school music extravaganza called the South Iowa Cedar League Honor Band Festival. Before the students from the various schools in the area performed together in one giant orchestra, their band instructors gave them a show, big band-style. Stephen had brought his saxophone, so he joined us. We played three songs to a packed gymnasium. It was great fun! Stephen's stay was, indeed, memorable.

Try as we might, we couldn't get Stephen a job within the publishing corporation. I wanted him to find employment and stay in Iowa. Since we were now good friends, it would have been nice if he lived closer.

Things worked out for him, however. When his stay with me came to an end, he went back to California and soon met the lady he would eventually marry. I guess fate wouldn't allow him to stay in Iowa when there was a future life-long partner waiting to meet him back in California.

Realizing I had acquired a lifetime friend because of my Frankie Laine avocation, I immediately, once again, took note of the scope of Frankie's celebrity. Quite literally, Frankie's fame allowed me to make contacts with people from all over the world. I wouldn't have had this opportunity otherwise. One of the duties of all writers in our corporation was to write an opinion column to be published in all the area weeklies owned by the corporation within Iowa County. Each of us rotated, and were responsible for a column every month or so. Since I was editor for the *North English Record,* I named my column "Record Scratches." We were allowed to write about almost anything we wanted. I decided to write a column about how I became friends with someone because of my Frankie Laine association. My article centered on the power of a published article—in this case, my Frankie Laine feature. Within my newspaper editorial, I reviewed my friendship with Stephen.

Requiring a human interest feature for the *North English Record,* I decided to write a condensed version of my original Frankie Laine article. When the rewrite was finished, the article filled almost an entire page in the newspaper, even though it was more concise than its predecessor. On March 6, 1997, the revamped article was published in three of the corporation's seven newspapers.

After being published, I sent Frankie a copy of the revised article. A few days later, I was at the corporation headquarters when I received a call from the secretary who worked at the office in North English. Excitedly, she informed me that Frankie had called for me, leaving a message on the voice mail system. She saved the message for me to listen to. Racing back to North English, I was elated over Frankie's message:

> *"Hi Craig—Frankie Laine. Just read the article all over again—brought back a lot of memories. Give me a call if you feel like talkin'. . . . Thanks a lot. Bye."*

I drove home and, before I lost my adrenaline rush, telephoned Frankie. His first words upon hearing my name were, "Hey, Craig, how the hell are ya!!" For me, this was a great icebreaker. Upon informing him I was glad he liked my article, Frankie said, "Yeah, it was wonderful."

He asked me how I was doing, and I answered that I was fine and extremely busy.

"Good, I'm glad to hear that," he replied with a sincere caring tone.

I wanted to know how he was doing. "Well, if everything goes along like this the way it has been for the last couple of months, I guess I'll be all right. Getting old ain't for sissies," he chuckled.

I pointed out to him that he's always young at heart, which segued into asking about his new album project. Ironically, he informed me that one of the songs to be included on the album was the standard classic "Young at Heart." (Soon thereafter, that album was released on CD as *Wheels of a Dream.*)

I informed Frankie of how Stephen and I met and became friends because of my initial Frankie Laine article. "That's marvelous," he responded.

Frankie suggested I try publishing my article nationally. We discussed a possibility, and he gave me a contact name and address. He asked me if I was going to stay in journalism. I informed him that I probably would until something more lucrative came along. During our telephone conversation, he eventually answered with the best advice I could have possibly received: "Do what you love to do because the money will come later." He signed off by asking me to say hello to Latisha.

I was in awe, and my whole body tingled with a pleasant shock after this phone conversation. I felt as close to Frankie as I had in 1985, both during and after our long visit. He was as insightful and jovial as he was during the realization of my initial quest.

* * *

The office for the *North English Record* was located in a building owned by Phil Tyrrell, a member of the Iowa House of Representatives who also operated a thriving insurance business. Phil strongly believed in the importance of a local newspaper. This conviction was so intense that he provided the town's newspaper editor with an office in his building, free of charge. For the first time in my life, I had my own office. Phil and I became great friends. He often spoke to me about his legislative career. He also opened my eyes to the possibility of obtaining a state job. He mesmerized me with this prospect. Excitedly, I asked him to inform me of any job openings at the Iowa State Capitol.

Shortly thereafter, much to my amazement, Phil came to me with details on an opening for a Legislative Information Officer. He obtained an application for me, and I immediately filled it out and sent it in along with my résumé. An interview at the Statehouse soon followed. Phil provided the legislative directors with a fine recommendation, which, no doubt, was a great influence.

A few days later, I received a telephone call from the Deputy Director of the Legislative Service Bureau informing me that the position was mine. I was both ecstatic and apprehensive. The new job meant eventually moving to Des Moines. This would be the first time I'd live a long distance from my daughter. Tish and I have always been a team. Even though I realized the miles between us wouldn't change this, there was still a pit in the bottom of my stomach.

I began as a Legislative Information Officer in December 1997. I will always be indebted to Phil, who, as far as I was concerned, was directly responsible for the best career move of my life.

Technology suddenly became rampant. While I was still in college in 1995, the Internet was in its infancy. Electronic mail was just beginning to become popular. Even though I worked on a computer throughout college and in my postgraduation newspaper career, I never truly delved into the Internet until I began working in Des Moines.

Upon discovering that one of the members of the Iowa House of Representatives was Dan Boddicker, I wondered if he was related to my late friend, Rick Boddicker. I sent Dan an e-mail, and he wrote back that he was, indeed, a relative. That's all it took for me to become friends with Dan, also a musician.

With my full introduction to e-mail, letter writing on paper became a thing of the past. Now keeping in touch with Stephen, Tony Cooper, and Helen Snow was accomplished electronically. Nonetheless, I have kept a file of letters and printed e-mails regarding my Laine avocation throughout my affiliation with Frankie Laine.

Because of my association with Frankie Laine, I have received many letters from all over the world. I've saved letters written to me from Frankie's admirers in Australia, Canada, Denmark, England, and Scotland. Of course, I also kept letters from those who love Frankie from many states in this country.

A couple of e-mail notes I received were very touching. In 1998, I received a note from a lady who wanted to know if I had a copy of "I Get Sentimental Over Nothing," recorded by Frankie in 1949. According to her, this was her mother and late father's love song. I sent her a copy of the song on audiocassette. After her mother heard the recording, this lady wrote back:

When she heard the song she cried—really cried.

Such is the effect Frankie Laine has on his admirers. Another lady sent me an e-mail bestowing upon me the obvious love she and her family have for Frankie:

Frankie Laine (the voice) was my father's favorite singer, and he even married my mother to the sound of "High Noon" back in 1962. As a thirty-four-year old, I have grown up listening to Frankie singing all his classics and have some great memories of my dad trying to emulate Frankie at many a happy family occasion.

Still another lady stated in her e-mail:

I'm an old admirer of Frankie Laine. Met him at the Blue Max in Chicago one evening in the 1970s. He must remember this night because I came with a girlfriend, and I brought a list of all his old recordings. This was the thrill of my life, just being able to speak to him and how very gracious he was to us.

Out of all the letters and e-mails I have received, the most touching came from a gentleman who had recently suffered a stroke behind one of his eyes. Doctors were fighting a losing battle in the attempt to save the sight in his other eye. I met this person electronically while purchasing an old Frankie Laine record he advertised on an Internet auction site. We communicated through e-mail. Upon discovering Frankie Laine and

I were friends, he asked me if I would consider asking Frankie for an autographed picture for him. I agreed to do this, sending Frankie a note right away. Frankie was happy to oblige and sent this man a personalized and autographed photo. Upon receiving Frankie's photo, this man's wife wrote to me:

> *His package arrived and it did wonders for him. What a day he had after receiving his picture from Frankie Laine!*

In a subsequent e-mail, she wrote:

> *He is losing his eyesight. Many times during the day he proudly sits and stares at his personalized autographed picture of Frankie Laine, while his world silently begins slipping into darkness.*

CHAPTER NINE

Projects

F rankie's secretary, Muriel Moore, died in November 1996. Immediately, I sent Frankie a letter with my sincere condolences. He wrote back:

> *Thank you so much for your kind letter of sympathy*
> *regarding the passing of Muriel. She was with me for 48*
> *years. It has been difficult, and I will miss her. She was*
> *wonderful and a dear friend.*

I'll never forget my excitement when Muriel first gave me Frankie's home phone number in 1985 so I could arrange my initial visit. I was glad to meet this fine lady and have my picture taken with her during Frankie's eightieth birthday party in 1993. She was such an important part of Frankie's life and career.

After Frankie announced that his new secretary would be Mary-Jo Coombs, I decided to acquaint myself with her by sending her a copy of my original Frankie Laine article. Her letter back to me set aside any doubt that she would be a fantastic secretary to Frankie. Mary-Jo wrote:

> *Dear Craig,*
>
> *Thank you so much for sending me your article on Frankie Laine. It's terrific! What a very special day you spent with him. And, he is a very special person, isn't he?—a true gentleman, a great man, and an unbeatable singer! It's an honor to be his secretary.*
>
> *I look forward to talking to you and seeing you.*
>
> *Best regards,*
>
> *Mary-Jo*

Both societies scheduled a big Frankie Laine eighty-fifth birthday party in San Diego for March 29 and 30, 1998. I contacted my friend Stephen Fratallone, and we made plans to get together. This would be his first attendance at a Frankie Laine birthday party and my second.

I booked a flight to San Diego and met Stephen and his new wife the day after I arrived. We spent a lot of time together because they had a car. We had a great time visiting the Cabrillo Monument and the Old Point Loma Lighthouse, as well as Tijuana. It was wonderful seeing Stephen again and getting to know his wife.

A party on Sunday, March 29, was a prelude to Frankie's birthday celebration. Members of both the English and American societies joined in the fun at an afternoon Mexican Fiesta in Frankie's honor. The festivities were held at the rehearsal hall of the Musicians' Association of San Diego County, Local 325 of the American Federation of Musicians. The fiesta included a Mexican buffet, a mariachi group, and, best of all, a brief concert by Frankie.

Frankie's conductor, Benny Hollman, brought in members of Frankie's backup orchestra and party attendees were treated to a Frankie Laine performance. I was overjoyed. The room was brightly lit, not the usual darkness of a nightclub or concert hall. Frankie sang only a few feet away from where I sat in the small room. The concert was very intimate and wonderful. Prior to the show, during the luncheon, Stephen shot some video footage of me chatting with Frankie. This was the second time I appeared on videotape with Frankie Laine.

I met Tony Cooper for the first time at this event. We had time to chat only briefly, but it was good to finally meet.

At this point, there had been three large birthday parties for Frankie that were attended by members of both societies. Every five years, beginning with Frankie's seventy-fifth birthday, a large birthday bash was held. During the Mexican Fiesta, Frankie provided medallions for each society member suspended on a red, white, and blue ribbon. Each medallion was emblazoned with the American society logo and featured Frankie's autograph. His birth date was also included. This medallion commemorated his eighty-fifth birthday. If members attended all three of the parties, their medallion inlays were gold-colored; if members attended two, their medallion inlays were silver-colored; and first-timers received bronze-colored medallion inlays. Mine was silver.

The following evening's festivities took place at the Half Moon Inn. Frankie's stream of well-wishers had grown since his eightieth birthday party took place there. What was more relaxing and intimate and only slightly crowded five years earlier was now jam-packed and boisterous.

Over the years I was privileged to meet more people within Frankie's circle, and visited with many of them. In addition to talking to Helen and Tony, I also met and chatted with Benny Hollman and Frankie's new secretary, Mary-Jo Coombs.

Many people had read my original Frankie Laine article, and I brought along copies for those who might want one.

Frankie was cordial but exhausted from this, the second party in two days. Stephen and I took each other's picture with Frankie. Stephen videotaped me chatting with members of both societies.

My dear Scottish friend, Norman Foster, also came to the party. He absolutely delighted me by asking if I would like a copy of the video he took during Frankie's eightieth birthday bash. "You and your daughter are on the tape quite a bit," he informed me in his Scottish brogue. "The tape also shows you visiting with Frankie and Nan," he added. I was stunned. For years I've mourned the fact my borrowed video camera failed to capture the events during Frankie's eightieth birthday party. Now, from seemingly out of nowhere, all the footage I missed did, indeed, exist! It brought back memories of when Helen Snow serendipitously videotaped Frankie's episode of *Bachelor Father*.

Norman became dear to my heart from that moment on. We are still great friends. Too bad we live so far from each other. What a joy it would be to have Norman close by. I later received the tape, and it was wonderful to relive the party that Tishie and I experienced together.

Again, I wished I had more time to chat with everyone. I brought along an autograph book and asked everyone I spoke with to sign it for me.

I was thrilled so many people from the English society were able to make it to the soirée. I met the FLIAS chairperson, Rosemary Carden, and I introduced myself to Paul Durham, editor of *Laine Lines*.

When Helen and I had the chance to chat again, she gave me information on a new Frankie Laine project. It was an album of newly recorded Frankie Laine songs due to be released. I felt privileged to be in on this inner circle "secret." Helen never failed to allow me to feel special within the world of Frankie Laine. When we finished our chat, I kissed her good-bye as I left. Little did I know at that time that this would be good-bye, forever.

I left the party fairly early in order to arrive at the airport for a late-night flight back home.

* * *

As inevitable as life, death, once again, struck the Frankie Laine group. In April 1998, Jimmy Namaro, Frankie's former pianist, arranger, and conductor, died of heart failure at age eighty-five. Introduced by Frankie at every show as the "Toronto Flash," Jimmy was always classy; he was special. Upon learning of his death, my thoughts immediately went back, once again, to the Christmas PSA taping in San Diego, when I sat next to Jimmy as he played "Silent Night" on his electric piano while Frankie sang.

Around the same time I received the news of Jimmy's death, I was at a nightclub in Cedar Rapids with some friends. One of the musicians in the band was an old pal of mine. It was in his studio that I recorded my album,

That Drummer! During the band's break I walked over to the bandstand and greeted my old friend.

"Where is Danny Aarhus these days?" I inquired as we shook hands.

"Oh, he's about six feet under in Center Point," was the reply in an obvious attempt to make light of a dreadful answer.

I was immediately numbed as the smile melted from my face. The last I'd heard, Danny was living in Hawaii. His mother lived in Center Point, Iowa. My friend explained that Danny, who had become a diabetic, allegedly went into insulin shock and died. Apparently living alone, his body wasn't discovered until a few days after he died, and authorities found it in a dreadful state. I couldn't believe that my old musician friend was gone. Like Rick, Danny was only in his forties. This was a tragic loss. I was feeling old. Danny and I had been through a lot together.

* * *

Moving on with my life, I turned, once again, to my avocation. I discovered David Miller on the Internet. His site, called *Swingin' Down the Lane,* featured jazz and big band musicians and singers, both past and contemporary. I sent an e-mail to David informing him of my association with Frankie. I asked him if he would be interested in publishing my original Frankie Laine feature article on his Internet site. He readily agreed. Because of its length, the article was subsequently placed on his site in three installments.

David enjoyed my article very much. Since he also hosted a radio show for National Public Radio, also called *Swingin' Down the Lane,* I hoped he would also be interested in interviewing Frankie for broadcast on the program. I assured David that I could provide all the contact information necessary to set up an interview with Frankie. David wrote back and was thrilled to have an opportunity to visit with such a music legend as Frankie Laine. As quickly as possible, I sent David information on how to get in touch with Frankie. He wasted no time setting up an interview.

Meanwhile, on May 8, 1998, Frankie was interviewed from his home in San Diego on Des Moines radio station WHO to promote his newly released CD, *Wheels of a Dream*. I decided to call in during the phone call portion of the program. After brief on-air introductions, I spoke:

> Craig: *"I think Frank remembers me from some of the times I went out to see him."*
>
> Frankie: *"Oh, yes, I remember very well."*
>
> Craig: *"How ya doing?"*
>
> Frankie: *"Pretty good. In fact I did an interview with somebody just a couple of days ago who came here on your say-so."*
>
> Craig: *"Yes, how'd that go?"*
>
> Frankie: *"Was that Dave Miller?"*
>
> Craig: *"Yes."*
>
> Frankie: *"Yeah, he was here yesterday."*
>
> Craig: *"Yes."*
>
> Frankie: *"And we did about an hour and a half. He said he was going to insert the music later."*
>
> Craig: *"Good deal."*
>
> Frankie: *"I don't know when he's gonna play it . . . ."*
>
> Craig: *"Well, he said he'd send me a copy. So when he does, I'll send you a copy of it."*

Frankie: *"Okay."*

Program Host: *"So what are you guys talking about?"*

Frankie: *"He's recommended somebody who was coming here for a visit to do an interview with me, and he was here yesterday. And, Craig's been a long-time fan."*

Program Host: *"Well, neat."*

Frankie: *"God, it goes back to what, Craig?"*

Craig: *"1985, Frankie."*

Frankie: *"'85?"*

Craig: *"I took a bus out to see you."*

Frankie: *"Yeah. And you stayed at the YMCA that night, 'cause you didn't have anyplace to stay."*

Craig: *"Right."*

Program Host: *"You're a groupie!"*

Craig: *"Yup."*

Frankie: *"I sent you home on a bus the next day."*

Craig: *"Yup. And you treated me just like a father* [would treat his son], *and I'll never forget that as long as I live. You're really precious to us all."*

Frankie: *"Well, thank you. And Dave was very nice. He did a marvelous interview. He's on a syndicated line of stations. He's on about forty stations. He says he has a tremendous listening audience. He's out of what—Little Rock?"*

Craig: *"Yes, Little Rock, Arkansas."*

> Program Host: *"Excellent. Hey, well, thank you so much,*
> *Craig, for calling up."*
> Frankie: *"Okay, Craig."*
> Craig: *"Yeah, Frank. Take care and I'll talk to you later."*
> Frankie: *"Talk to you later. Bye."*
> Program Host: *"Bye, bye."*

Our brief radio chat was wonderful. It endeared me to Frankie every time I spoke to him. He always knew who I was. Because of this, I felt we were truly friends. What a great connection I had with Frankie! It is a wonderful feeling to know that such an important music legend of the twentieth century thought well of me. Surely my step was lighter that day, my head held higher.

Frankie, a musical trend setter, was emulated time and again by famous singers who followed in his footsteps. Frankie is one of a kind. Singers like Tony Bennett, among many others, owe a musical debt to Frankie. This is the same Frankie Laine who is now my special friend! Not only did Frankie Laine make me feel good through his stylistic, passionate singing renditions, but he possesses the unique ability to also make me feel good about myself.

Soon thereafter, I sent Frankie a sympathy card regarding the death of Jimmy Namaro. He wrote back thanking me for the card and related how sorry he also was to hear of Jimmy's passing. Frankie wrote:

> He was a good friend and marvelous arranger and composer.

In the same letter, Frankie also related how good it was to talk with me on WHO.

Early in May, I received an e-mail back from David Miller.

What a wonderful visit I had! He [Frankie] *remembers your visit fondly, and that's partly why he was so cordial to me, I'm sure . . . . Thanks for making it all possible!!!*

As promised, I received an audio copy of the radio program *Swingin' Down the Lane*, featuring Frankie, from David. David made sure that I was given credit over the airwaves for making the interview with Frankie possible. He also pointed out during the program that he had asked me what my favorite song of Frankie's is. He recounted that I answered it was difficult to choose one, but if I did, it would be "Give Me a Kiss for Tomorrow." Then he featured Frankie's recording of this song in my honor.

I followed through with my promise to Frankie and sent him a copy of the program. He wrote me a letter thanking me for the copy and also expressing gratitude, once again, for writing the article, which he credited with spawning David's interest in conducting the interview.

I was pleased to set things in motion for Frankie. Hopefully, I was doing my part to help promote Frankie's latest work, *Wheels of a Dream*. I wrote an article entitled "Swingin' with Frankie Laine" exclusively for the FLSOA newsletter, and it was published that summer. The article featured my association with David Miller.

I thought seriously about producing my own radio program featuring Frankie and his music. After all, I have a broadcasting degree. I had mentioned this to Frankie in a previous letter. He wrote back that he'd be glad to be interviewed for my new concept radio program, and he granted me permission to call him anytime.

My idea was to provide a Frankie Laine program featuring some of the recordings he made that nobody has heard before. Fabulous tunes that never made the charts. My program would highlight Frankie at his best. I started to work on writing a script while attempting to generate interest with various Iowa radio stations. Most importantly, I required a radio studio to produce the program. My friend Dan Boddicker, helped me find such a radio station—KROS in Clinton, Iowa. I contacted the station's general manager, Don Schneider. Dan knew Don quite well and gave an excellent recommendation on my behalf. My hard sell to Don was included in a letter. In it I stated that the recent death of Frank Sinatra reminds us music lovers that our "golden age" musical entertainers are rapidly becoming extinct. In my opinion, the importance of doing something that is part of this musical legacy—while the entertainer is still with us—is monumental. There are so few of these special persons left. We must treasure the ones still here.

Don telephoned me, and I informed him of my plans for structuring a program on Frankie. He was excited and figured the program would go over well with his listening audience. I made arrangements to meet him at his station one hundred twenty miles away.

I worked diligently on creating a script that briefly explained Frankie's history and updated listeners on his current career. Most importantly, I featured the music Frankie recorded that is unfamiliar to most listeners. In order to come up with a list of songs to use, I thought about Frankie's vast array of emotions. Utilizing song categories based upon certain emotions was the key I searched for to tie the script together. I developed seven categories in which I considered the order of relevance, roughly based upon my emotion idea—rhythmical, emotional, dramatic, romantic, exciting, inspirational, and spiritual. I deemed these categories to be the essential Frankie Laine. Other than Frankie, I can't think of any other singer who can be categorized in as many areas of passion.

Basically, all other singers perform in one style. If they stray into other genres, for example cowboy songs, they still maintain the same sound and style. Frankie's unique talent allows for changes in style. He magically transforms himself into the type of singer listeners imagine should be singing a particular song. If he sings a cowboy tune, Frankie's voice is portrayed on the canvas of the mind as a rugged or range-weary cowpoke. He allows listeners to believe he is the real thing. When he sings jazz, the cowboy disappears altogether and a jazz or blues singer emerges with as much truth and believability. Only an amazing talent is able to pull this off. What a musical genius Frankie Laine is! I knew this, and the goal of my project was to relate this to the listening audience. "Project" seemed to be a marvelous description for the labor of love I ultimately created. I entitled the program *The Laine Project*.

Unfortunately, since I didn't have all the Frankie Laine songs I wanted to use on CD, I also used both records and tapes from my collection and decided to put everything on audiocassette tape in the order I'd feature the material. I also compiled a list of Frankie's gold records and, in chronological order, recorded snippets of each. The reasoning behind doing this was to familiarize listeners with Frankie by featuring songs by him they could relate to. Appreciation for the obscure Frankie Laine songs would follow. Finally, I had a script written.

I set up a date with KROS radio in October 1998. Upon my arrival, Don brought me into a broadcast room. I went to work setting up my material and finalizing my script. "You do the announcing, and I'll run the controls on the board," Don instructed.

I had previously called Frankie to set up an interview for this day, which was scheduled to be recorded for insertion into my program. All was ready. I had also scheduled two newspaper photographers from two different area newspapers to arrive at the studio and take pictures of me talking into the microphone. A few days before actually recording my production, reporters from both newspapers interviewed me. I hoped this publicity might spur a further interest in listening to the program once the radio previews were aired.

My program was assembled on tape before actually airing. This is the way I wanted it presented. I began *The Laine Project* by speaking over the intro to Frankie's Columbia recording of "Wonderful Wasn't It?":

> *"Welcome to 'The Laine Project.' I'm your host, Craig Cronbaugh. During this program we're featuring the wonderful music and vocal stylings of the wonderful Frankie Laine."*

After this spoken introduction, the song plays in its entirety.

I telephoned Frankie at his home at the appointed time. He answered all my questions as Don recorded our conversation for the program. One of the most personal and touching moments for me was when I asked Frankie to dedicate one of his old recorded songs, "My Little One," to Latisha from me. This he did. I was later criticized by others for this move. Seemingly this introduction was too personal an approach used for my own benefit. I did this as a tribute to my daughter. This also further proved to be a testament not only to a great entertainer, but to an approachable, caring man. What's wrong with demonstrating love? Only cynics have a problem with it. This was, after all, my time, talents, and money at work. This was *my* project. I wrote, produced, directed, and hosted it. I accomplished all this to demonstrate to others what a great entertainer Frankie Laine is. "Love" is the key word. My utmost priority was sharing this love with others, for their enjoyment. I never wanted nor received a dime for any of it.

Within my collection was a cassette tape of two songs Frankie recorded many years ago, which were never released. These were the same two songs the FLSOA president, Jerry Massengill, had sent me in 1985. One of the songs, entitled "Brandy Dreams," became one of my favorite Frankie Laine recordings. Since *The Laine Project* featured great Frankie Laine tunes seldom heard on the airwaves, I decided to introduce that particular song in my production. I figured this would add even more value to my program. During my phone interview with Frankie, I asked his permission to include "Brandy Dreams." He gladly gave his consent. He also answered a question regarding this song during the interview.

Like any major project, something's bound to go wrong and my program was no exception. Frankie's end of the telephone interview recorded well. However, the audio volume on my voice was recorded too low. Unfortunately, since it was discovered after my interview with Frankie was completed, nothing could be done to remedy this. Our only alternative was to record my questions over and attempt to make them sound as if I was speaking directly to Frankie. This was difficult to do, not to mention extremely time-consuming, but somehow we pulled it off. The outcome was a clean "studio" question segment and a telephone reply by Frankie.

The Laine Project was recorded on four reels of audiotape. After an exhausting day of recording the program, I drove home in a thunderstorm—tired but happy. A couple of days later, Don informed me that one of the reels of tape used for the program was warped and would have to be rerecorded. I was crushed! There was no alternative—I had to reschedule studio time. I made arrangements with Don to redo that portion of the program.

Upon returning to KROS, I listened to some of the songs on the other tapes and decided to further boost the audio by rerecording them. In addition to performing the one reel over, I also revamped the rest of the audio. Later, to my chagrin, I discovered one of the other reels had been utilized to capacity and should not have been used for the program. *Damn! This is becoming a nightmare! Why didn't we use virgin tape?!*

The resulting fidelity was not as high-quality as the other reels. This produced a rather awkward audio volume drop within the program when that particular reel was played. Small radio stations don't have large budgets and therefore reuse their audiotapes. Looking back, I should have personally bought new reels of tape for my program. Taking it for granted that the station would assume responsibility for both the electronics and mechanics was my oversight.

The finished program ran approximately two hours. Don dubbed the entire project onto two cassette tape masters. I took the tapes to a recording studio in Des Moines and paid to have the audio painstakingly edited and equalized through an elaborate computer system. The finished product was burned onto two CDs. Thus, *The Laine Project* was completed.

The Laine Project aired three times on KROS and another time on KMAQ in Maquoketa, Iowa. I previously generated an interest in KMAQ station manager Leighton Hepker, and he also agreed to air the program. Dan Boddicker was responsible for informing KMAQ about my program, as well. He really put forth the effort allowing *The Laine Project* to both become reality and enter the airwaves.

The radio stations that aired my program were small, but they did broadcast *The Laine Project,* and many people heard it and enjoyed it. My goal was fulfilled.

I mailed Frankie the front page of my script for *The Laine Project* to autograph for me. I also sent him copies of the CDs. When I called him after he'd had a chance to listen, he seemed pleased that what I had accomplished made me happy. He was also very appreciative. The program now belongs to the ages and occupies a special place within my Frankie Laine collection.

Ironically, Dan was becoming my best friend, just as his relative Rick had been in earlier days. Dan had previously written a song entitled "Epiphany." He asked me if I thought Frankie might like to record the song. I contacted Frankie to ask if he might be interested in recording Dan's tune. Frankie asked me to send him a CD copy of the song. Dan had formerly recorded his song on audiocassette, so all he had to do was copy it to a CD.

Within a few days I received a message on my home telephone answering machine from Mary-Jo Coombs, asking me to call Frankie.

When I phoned him, he seemed interested in perhaps recording Dan's song. He asked to have Dan call him. I couldn't wait to telephone Dan and tell him the news. "Call me back as soon as you're finished speaking with Frankie," I instructed. When Dan called me back, he informed me that Frankie had given him many songwriting pointers, and he had asked him to have "Epiphany" transferred into sheet-music form by a copyist. A few days later, Dan had his song ready for Frankie and mailed it to him.

Time marched onward and, unfortunately, Frankie never recorded the song. Dan is forever grateful nonetheless, and he loves the fact that Frankie even considered recording his song.

In August 1998, a couple of months prior to producing *The Laine Project,* I received an alarming e-mail from Helen Snow:

> *Hi, Craig:*
>
> *Right now I have been having nothing but tests and more tests. Next week sometime I should have all the results back. Have to go September 1st for a biopsy. Doctors think my condition is serious.*

She closed by asking me not to tell anyone within Frankie's circle about her news. Of course, I honored her request. On September 3, 1998, I received information from Helen that saddened me. She informed me that her biopsy revealed terminal lung cancer and that specialists didn't foresee much hope for her recovery. When I told my friend Dan about this, he recommended that I tell Helen about a person he knew who gave new hope to the terminally ill. I contacted Helen and pleaded with her to telephone this person, but she refused. She informed me she was content to go along with God's bidding.

Helen's e-mail of February 1, 1999, was shocking. In it she described the pain she was in from a recent removal of her cancerous lung as well as the removal of her entire right kidney.

Trying not to worry too much about Helen, I began an e-mail communication with Mary Garland from California. She informed me that she was also a Frankie Laine fan. Her late father had been a huge fan, and she understandably picked up on his enchantment. One of her first notes described her father's obvious love for Frankie:

> *I grew up listening to Frankie Laine, as I think my father was his biggest fan. When my father passed away not too long ago, he left me all his albums . . . .*
>
> *I remember once Frankie gave a concert at the Bakersfield Business Conference, and I bought a ticket for my father, and he was so thrilled! He told me that he wished I had gone with him, but the tickets were expensive at the time, and I could only afford one. I was really glad he went because he talked about that up until the day he passed away.*

Mary and I became good friends because we both admire Frankie Laine and love his music. I happily contemplated both my most recent male and female personal Frankie Laine friends. *Too bad they live in California.* I sent Mary copies of all my Frankie Laine projects. We loved writing about our favorite singer and chatting on the telephone. Eventually, we decided to meet in California and visit Frankie in person. Our plan was for me to introduce Mary to Frankie.

As quickly as I was making a new friend, I was losing an old one. One of the last correspondences I received from Helen Snow was an e-mail on March 3, 1999. She stated that she was feeling dizzy and had experienced both slurred speech and a headache for a week. Her oncologist subsequently discovered two cancerous tumors in her head. Helen was walking with a cane and getting ready for seventeen weeks of radiation. I was very sad.

* * *

Moving on with my avocation, in the spring of 1999, I persuaded IPTV, the Iowa public broadcasting system, to produce a feature for television regarding my Frankie Laine association and collection. The PBS station was scheduling a program highlighting various Iowa collectors. They deemed it appropriate to add my Frankie Laine collection to their list.

With a feature promised by IPTV, I immediately contacted the *Involvement Magazine,* asking editor Jane Bigbee if she would write an article regarding the feature and its creation. Jane was more than happy to oblige. "This will make a great follow-up to your 1995 Frankie Laine article," she eagerly envisioned.

A camera operator and the feature producer, Jack Shepard, arrived at my home on a windy spring day. The feature was scheduled to run on both May 7 and May 9, 1999, during IPTV's collectors' program. Despite the fact the feature was slated to be only four minutes in length, it literally took all day to videotape both my interview and various parts of my Frankie Laine collection. The photographer for the magazine article was also busy taking various pictures during the interviewing process.

Since I owned an old record and radio console that played 78s, I suggested they shoot a scene showing an old 78 spinning and juxtapose this with the scene from Frankie's 1950 Columbia movie *When You're Smiling,* in which there is a close-up of a similar record and radio console with a record spinning on the turntable as Frankie begins singing "Georgia on My Mind." Jack liked the idea, and they videotaped it as I suggested.

I allowed Jack to take several videotapes from my collection back to the studio to use for the feature. I also suggested they use the footage of Frankie and me chatting at the 1998 Mexican Fiesta, which Stephen had taped for me. My idea was to add this footage in slow motion for a dramatic effect.

One of the more thought-provoking things I said during my interview regarding a celebrity career collection unexpectedly popped into my head:

> *"Once you actually meet the person you're collecting,*
> *it's great. I mean, imagine collecting Superman magazines*
> *and actually getting to meet Superman."*

Jack wanted to center a portion of the feature around *The Laine Project.* Somehow, he wanted me to simulate speaking into a microphone while reading my script. I came up with the idea of using a real studio. The studio where *The Laine Project* was electronically and digitally remastered would provide the perfect setting. The idea appealed to Jack.

The next day, I contacted the studio manager and explained my plan for using the studio for our production. He was happy to oblige, so I made an appointment for us to tape our segment.

When we all gathered at the studio to tape the scene, I read the beginning of my script while the videographer taped me from different angles. I was seated in front of a professional microphone that closely resembled the type used in radio. Shots of the control board with the engineer's hands sliding the controls added extra authenticity. The result was believable footage of me performing *The Laine Project*.

When the production was finished, Jack sent me an e-mail informing me that I was welcome to drive to the IPTV studio and view the feature before it aired. I couldn't wait to see it. When I arrived, Jack took me into a production booth and ran my four-minute feature, now entitled *Memory Laine*. Both of my scene ideas had been incorporated into the production. When the screening of this production was finished, I had tears in my eyes. "That's the best compliment I can get," Jack responded.

The article regarding *Memory Laine* was published in the May 1999 issue of the *Involvement Magazine*.

Memory Laine aired two times in 1999 and several more times since. Later, Jack informed me that *Memory Laine* was considered by IPTV to be one of their best and favorite short features.

My happiness upon completing *Memory Laine* was soon diminished by a keen sadness. The FLSOA newsletter front page for October and November 1999 read:

> *Helen Snow*
>
> *It is with sadness that I have to inform you that Helen passed away on August 12, 1999, of cancer. Helen had been battling cancer for some time. It was her request to keep her health condition private.*
>
> *Helen became president of the fan club in 1985. She was a devoted fan of Frank since she was a teenager. Through her hard work she kept fans informed on Frank's*

activities and music. She also kept local disc jockeys
supplied with the same information and recordings. . . .
She will be missed by all.

I lost my fellow Frankie Laine collector. I lost a friend. Helen colored my life. She allowed me into the Frankie Laine circle, treating me with unequivocal respect throughout our friendship. Our mutual love of Frankie Laine and his music developed further into a love that two friends share for each other. I will always miss Helen.

I sent my condolences regarding Helen to Frankie. He replied in a letter:

Yes, I was sorry to hear of Helen Snow's passing. She
certainly was a good friend for a long time. I appreciated
all she did as president of the fan club . . . .

* * *

Mary and I both arrived in San Diego in November and telephoned Mary-Jo Coombs to meet with us prior to our prearranged visit with Frankie. Mary-Jo, Frankie's devoted executive secretary, is a wonderful person. She is extremely dedicated to her Frankie Laine work and loved hearing our Frankie Laine stories.

On November 12, 1999, we greeted Frankie and his new wife, Marcia, at their home. It brought back a lot of pleasant memories to be in Frankie's house again. Frankie and Marcia were married on June 5, 1999. I realized Marcia was a gal after my own heart when the first thing she did when she saw me was run over and shake my hand exclaiming, "I just have to meet you after reading your Frankie Laine article!" It seemed a friend of hers received the *Involvement Magazine* and shared the article with Marcia, long before she married Frankie. What a small world!

I discovered new treasures in Frankie's home. On one of his walls there is a picture of President John F. Kennedy, personally autographed to Frankie. Frankie's home is reminiscent of a museum of fascinating possessions. As I first saw in 1985, Frankie's collection of mule knickknacks, sent to him over the years by fans paying tribute to his big million-seller "Mule Train," was still proudly displayed.

During our visit, Frankie spoke about his friendship with the late Mario Lanza. I was fascinated because I'm a huge Lanza fan. Mario Lanza did a great Frankie Laine impersonation in one of his movie musicals in 1958 for MGM entitled *Seven Hills of Rome*. Wow! What stories! I was in heaven! During his reminiscing, I could tell how troubled Frankie was because Mario Lanza was a man in constant turmoil.

As we talked about certain celebrities, I asked Frankie if he ever knew George Burns. Frankie informed me that many years ago both George Burns and Jack Benny were close friends of his. George Burns was always a hero of mine. It seemed to me that Frankie certainly knew all the celebrities from the golden age of show business.

Excitedly, Frankie beckoned me to his music room. This was the same room where, in 1985, I wrote down record song titles while Frankie took his nap. "I want you to hear something," he said. He motioned me to a chair behind a desk. I sat down. Displayed on the wall directly behind me was Frankie's gold record, "Mule Train." "I want you to hear a jazz song I recently recorded. I think you'll really like it," Frankie chirped. Like an excited kid, Frankie played "Old Man Jazz" for me. In various parts of the song, he sang along. It was great to hear a new Frankie Laine recording. It was unknown to me then, but during the following year, I would feature that very song on a jazz radio station in Iowa.

Along with all the stuff I had Frankie sign for me, I also brought along a video camera and a previously written list of questions. I asked Frankie if he would allow me to conduct an interview. He acquiesced with a smile. Mary videotaped me interviewing Frankie.

During the interview, I asked Frankie what artist(s) influenced him the most. He chose Nat "King" Cole because of his singing style, as well as Billie Holiday. These two great singers were also among my all-time favorites. Frankie added that his late partner, Carl Fischer, was his greatest influential working partner. He cited the song they co-wrote, "We'll Be Together Again," which has become a famous jazz classic.

I asked Frankie who he would choose if he could meet any person living or dead. He didn't hesitate and thoroughly surprised me by choosing Jesus Christ.

I asked him to name his favorite recording, and he answered "I Believe," his best-seller; "That's My Desire," because it started his fame; and "That Lucky Old Sun," which redefined him from being known as strictly a jazz singer to a singer who could perform other genres of music. He also spoke about CD releases in the works, his Internet site, and his upcoming weekly springtime engagement in the Palm Springs Follies in 2000.

In addition to agreeing to sign more than a few old 78s, pieces of sheet music, and album covers I brought along, I was certainly very grateful to Frankie that day for allowing me to interview him, as well. He also graciously signed a CD set of *The Laine Project* for me. I felt fortunate accomplishing such a project about an artist and acquiring *that* artist's signature on the finished work.

Earlier that year, Mary showed me a letter she received from Frankie dated July 12, 1999. In it, he wrote:

> *Craig is a very dear long-time friend of mine. I hope*
> *he has told you the story of our first meeting. He is a great*
> *promoter of Frankie Laine music. He's special.*

The letter warmed my heart.

Mary and I are still friends and keep in touch. I'm glad that it was me who introduced her to her father's favorite singer.

* * *

During the 2000 Iowa Presidential Primary, I discovered Dan Rather would be broadcasting his CBS Evening News from the Iowa State Capitol Law Library. Prior to the broadcast on a Sunday afternoon, I drove to the Capitol to meet him.

I wanted to meet Rather because of my radio and television journalism studies in college. Arriving at the perfect time, I met him in the Law Library a few minutes before airtime. He was very cordial. When I informed him that his book, *The Camera Never Blinks,* was suggested reading in one of my broadcast classes in college, he was thrilled. I eagerly acknowledged that I regarded him as the modern day Edward R. Murrow. "Oh, thank you so much, Craig," he humbly replied.

I presented him with a copy of my original Frankie Laine article. "I want to tell you a little story about Frankie Laine," he surprised me by saying. As we stood there face to face, he detailed the time several years earlier when he and some of his friends attended a Frankie Laine concert in Texas.

"After the show we went backstage to meet Frankie," he explained. "Frankie was very nice to us."

Upon finishing his story, he asked me a favor.

"The next time you see Frankie, would you give him my best wishes?"

I promised I would. Soon, it was time for him to prepare for his live broadcast.

Through my job at the Capitol, I also became friends with Representative John Connors. John, a senior member of the Iowa House of Representatives, shared my love for jazz and popular singers of the 1940s and 1950s.

John introduced me to famed pianist Roger Williams, who visited the Capitol on March 6, 2000. Roger, who grew up in Des Moines, was back for an appearance on IPTV during the public television station's fundraising festival.

Roger attended school with John, and they were old friends. John always referred to Roger as "Louie" because his given name is Louis Weertz.

Prior to the famous piano player's visit, John proposed to the Iowa House of Representatives that Williams be presented with an honorary resolution commemorating his many achievements. The House joyfully consented. In order to present him with the resolution, John had asked him to attend a brief ceremony at the Capitol.

When I discovered Roger Williams was going to be in the House Chamber, I was determined to be there. I arrived at the chamber, and as soon as he was able to do so, John introduced me.

"Louie, this is my friend, Craig Cronbaugh," John began.

"Hi, Craig," Roger replied, flashing his famous toothy smile while shaking my hand.

"Craig and Frankie Laine are friends," John added.

"That's great," Roger responded. "You know I spoke with Frankie on the telephone a short time ago. What a grand old gentleman he is."

I found myself wondering what subject matter brought Roger and Frankie together over the telephone. Most likely, it was music-related.

A grand piano, previously brought in and placed in the chamber, now majestically awaited its master. Roger soon took to the keys and golden notes enchanted the entire body of the Iowa House and the many others crowded in for the brief concert. I was riveted as I watched. Listening to this great artist perform was wonderful. I especially enjoyed his trademark song, "Autumn Leaves."

Three years later, the office where I work became interested in purchasing some of Roger's CDs to sell. This sales project was part of a feature commemorating world-famous musical artists originally from Iowa. My goal was to purchase a quantity of CDs featuring Roger Williams and ask him to personally autograph them for us.

When asked, John dutifully supplied me with Roger's contact information. Twice, I had the pleasure of talking to Roger on the telephone from his home in California.

My second call to Roger, on July 15, 2003, was more conversational than the first. At one point during our chatter I casually mentioned that my birthday was approaching in a few days. Upon hearing this news, Roger thoroughly surprised me by plunking a few notes of "Happy Birthday" on his piano. I was extremely appreciative of this very kind gesture. It was as if I'd received a special birthday gift from Roger. *Wait until I tell my friends the great pianist Roger Williams played "Happy Birthday" for me on his piano!*

Roger exudes such happiness and contentment. His uplifting spirit is addictive. He is truly inspiring. During this same telephone conversation, I mentioned to him how stimulating his cheerful demeanor was. Roger responded with some great advice:

"Craig, you gotta learn how to laugh when life throws you a roadblock. You must laugh about it and not take it seriously when you feel you're beating your head against the wall over something. If you always take these things seriously, you'll die. Nobody is immune from life's stumbling blocks and all the crap that can come your way. It happens to everybody."

As far as I was concerned, I'd just received my second birthday gift from Roger Williams.

* * *

John Connors co-hosted a jazz radio program with Ford Roberts on Des Moines radio station KRNT. In March 2000, I asked him about the possibility of producing a show featuring Frankie Laine as guest. I felt sure I could obtain permission from Frankie to do a telephone interview for the program.

John was enthusiastic and set things up with the radio station. It so happened that Frankie's recently recorded song entitled "Old Man Jazz," the same song he played for me in his music room at home in 1999, still hadn't been released.

I wrote to Frankie, asking if I could feature that song on our radio production, and he agreed to send me a tape of the song. I was thrilled because this was an unreleased jazz work featuring Frankie Laine. What a great selling point for the radio show. He also agreed to be interviewed for the program.

As usual, Frankie delighted me yet again by sending me his own copy of the song on cassette tape with the title written in his own hand, sort of a junk tape we musicians keep a plethora of. I truly had an original and unique collector's item in my possession.

All segments for the radio program project were taped in advance. I telephoned Frankie in his room just prior to his performance run in the Palm Springs Follies. He was trying his best to conserve his voice for his upcoming string of performances. At the time I spoke with him, rehearsals were slated to begin for this gig. Frankie's voice was not holding out too well, and he was somewhat skeptical about completing this several-week engagement. Even his speaking voice sounded somewhat weak. I spoke with him briefly regarding "Old Man Jazz." When my part was finished, John conversed with Frankie. This telephone interview, combined with the debut of "Old Man Jazz" and a couple of older Laine recordings, completed the segment. The program aired on KRNT on April 1, 2000.

With the new decade in full swing, I was very satisfied with my station within the Frankie Laine group. Many times I analyzed my Frankie Laine avocation in my head. *I have really enjoyed myself and have created some good career-promoting projects for Frankie. Even though they're local productions, they made it possible for people in Iowa to rediscover Frankie Laine.*

I was soon to discover that my life would, once again, make an abrupt change for the better.

CHAPTER TEN
Up Among the Stars

They say that during a person's lifetime, some extreme event will happen that will totally change their life. This happened to me when I was involved in the car accident. No longer did I play music in a band. A college career became my goal. After college, I went into the newspaper business. Because of my career major in communications and electronic broadcasting, I became interested in delving into radio and television with my Frankie Laine avocation as my subject. While in college, I also studied the science of government. This prepared me for my new career at the Iowa State Capitol. All of this was a far cry from playing drums in a band.

Next to the birth of my daughter, the most important and happy situation in my life came in April 2000. I met Marlene Lockey, who would become my wife a year and a half later. I had placed an ad on the Internet, hoping to find a permanent relationship. Because I was having no luck finding someone using this method, I intended to delete my ad after checking it one final time. As fate would have it, Marlene had written to me. I'm thankful everyday for waiting to check my ad one last time, before removing myself from the electronic marketplace of the relationship seekers.

Marlene and I met in person for the first time at a downtown Des Moines restaurant. She and I both felt that we had finally found the person we needed in life and that our searching was over. *Life is good.*

When I first saw Marlene, she was walking toward the door to the restaurant. I was there waiting inside for her and watching out the window. The first thing I noticed, besides her being tall, was her long, beautiful brown hair blowing in the wind as she opened the door. We walked to a booth and sat down. As she looked at me I noticed how big and gorgeous her eyes were. She possessed a smile that lit up the room. We talked about our mutual lives, interests, and families. Soon, we decided to go for a walk together.

A short time after meeting Marlene, I discovered that a video documentary on the life and career of Frankie Laine was in the works. For some reason, I knew in my heart I needed to be a part of this documentary.

I contacted Mary-Jo Coombs and asked her for information on the documentary. She informed me that James Marino, who operated his own California-based video production company, JFM International Productions, Incorporated, would be producing the documentary.

"I must be a part of this documentary because I love Frankie so much," I declared to Mary-Jo.

"I'll ask Jimmy to give you a call," she replied.

"Thanks so much, Mary-Jo," I gratefully responded.

Mary-Jo always comes through for me. I don't know how I functioned within the Frankie Laine cluster for so long before she came aboard.

Jimmy Marino called me at work soon after my conversation with Mary-Jo. He asked me questions about my association with Frankie and my reasons for wanting to become a part of the documentary. "Because I'm his biggest fan, and I feel I should be in the documentary," I replied in an uncharacteristically narcissistic fashion. I really don't know why I used such a tactic. I guess I was utilizing an "all or nothing" approach at the possibility of being a part of this production. Therefore, I went "all out." Jimmy seemed interested enough to agree to look at some of my Frankie Laine productions. I informed him I would gladly come to San Diego, if he decided to interview me for the documentary.

After reviewing my Frankie Laine articles and my IPTV feature, Jimmy called me and notified me how impressed he was with my material and that he would very much like to interview me for Frankie Laine's story. We immediately made plans for me to visit San Diego in July, after he returned from England.

Marlene and I decided to travel to San Diego together. We'd make a vacation out of it and take full advantage of the beach while there.

Another mini quest I embarked upon during this period was to be photographed with all of Iowa's still-living former governors. To my delight, I discovered that former Governor Leo Hoegh, who served from 1955 to 1957, was still alive and living in Colorado Springs. *What a wonderful opportunity it would be if I could meet with him on our way out to California.* My enthusiasm was dampened upon telephoning the governor's home. His nurse answered, informing me that he was seriously ill and had brain cancer. She added that his doctors didn't expect him to live much longer. According to the nurse, the governor was not able to recognize people or speak. I really felt sad.

I figured it was fate that we should meet, primarily because in my Frankie Laine collection I have an old radio program entitled *Stars for Defense,* which Frankie guest-hosted. This radio show was produced during the era when there were various announcements to the public regarding the use of fallout shelters in the case of a nuclear attack. After leaving the Iowa governorship, Hoegh became director of the Office of Civil and Defense Mobilization in the Eisenhower Administration. During breaks within this particular radio program, former Governor Hoegh spoke about civil defense.

Possessing a taped radio program with both Frankie Laine and former Governor Leo Hoegh on the same broadcast was ironic, considering we planned to visit the governor on our way to San Diego before learning of his rapidly declining health. The fact that this governor was in office the year both Marlene and I were born added to the irony. (During our brief stay in San Diego, Marlene and I discovered that Governor Hoegh had died.)

* * *

I set up my interview for the documentary with Jimmy for July 17, 2000. I asked Jimmy if he could possibly arrange for us to visit with Frankie while we were there. I yearned to spend time with my famous friend again, and I also wanted Marlene to meet him. Jimmy cordially set everything up for us to come to Frankie's home after completing my interview. It was wonderful to finally meet Jimmy when he arrived at our motel to videotape.

We conducted the interview in our room. Jimmy asked me to relate the story of my first meeting with Frankie. With the camera rolling, I recounted my story and spoke about my feelings for Frankie Laine and his music. Prior to the interview, the front desk of the motel called our room, informing me that the electricity would soon be shut off in order to do some maintenance work. We would have only a few minutes to conduct the interview. *Just what I need—more pressure!*

A couple of minutes after the completion of my interview, the electricity was turned off. We'd just made it! Jimmy seemed enthused. "The interview went great," he proclaimed. He was also excited about the documentary in general. Jimmy divulged his admiration of Frankie Laine's vast career and related how lucky we all are to be able to personally know a man who has accomplished so much during his dynamic career and whose profession encompassed working with so many great celebrity legends. As he left, Jimmy promised to call Frankie and let him know we were on our way to his house for the scheduled visit.

Marlene and I drove to Frankie's area of San Diego. We never regretted renting a car during our visit within the city by the sea. Frankie's home is surrounded by a security gate, and I punched in his entry number at the telephone located near the entrance.

"Yeah," Frankie's voice responded.

"It's Craig Cronbaugh," I nervously replied.

Without a further word, the gate magically swung open, and we drove up the hill to the Laine residence.

Frankie seemed happy to see us. "I just got off the phone with Jimmy, and he said the interview went great," Frankie said.

I greeted Frankie with a hug and introduced him to Marlene.

"You have good taste," he said as he grinned at me.

Frankie took us on a brief tour of his house so Marlene could see it. As he showed us around, I pointed out to Marlene where certain events took place as depicted in my original Frankie Laine article. We followed Frankie out to his patio. Before sitting down, Marlene videotaped Frankie and me walking side by side with our arms around each other. What that great and wonderful man puts up with is remarkable. He certainly didn't have to go to all this trouble, but he happily did. He loves all his fans. All his fans adore him. With my adrenaline flowing I inadvertently overlooked Latisha, my family, and Marlene, when I informed Frankie, on-camera, that I loved him more than anyone in the world. "Except her," he replied with a smile, as he pointed to Marlene.

While we were getting ready to mug for the camera and Marlene was setting up the shot at the other end of the patio, Frankie turned to me and said, "She's beautiful. You've got good taste!" Again, Frankie was right on!

We enjoyed a wonderful chat on the patio. I looked over to my left where Frankie sat next to me and again experienced the feeling of awe and splendor in the realization that I was sitting this close to a legend of music. Frankie still had this effect on me and always will. One of the interesting things Frankie told us while on the patio was that his recording of "Cool Water" is one of Michael Jackson's favorite songs.

Before venturing back inside the house, we took pictures. Frankie's wife, Marcia, joined us and snapped a photo of Marlene, Frankie, and me together.

Once back in the house, Marlene delighted in playing with Marcia and Frankie's poodle, Matt. I think she held a special affection for this little guy for two reasons. Marlene's only son's name is Matt, and the first time Marlene saw what I looked like was from a picture of Matt, the poodle, and me taken when I was at the Laine residence in 1999.

As promised, I relayed the message to Frankie from Dan Rather. Frankie smiled as I gave him Rather's "best wishes."

Too soon, it was time for us to depart. One thing I am always conscious of is not overstaying my welcome when visiting Frankie. As we were saying our good-byes, Frankie gave Marlene a hug and delighted me by saying to her, "You take care of him; he's a good guy."

A few weeks after the trip to San Diego, I received an e-mail from Jimmy Marino asking me to get in touch with him:

> *Craig,*
>
> *How ya doing? I have a situation I want to pass by you. Before I give you the details, I want to know if you would be interested in helping me by utilizing the writing skills you seem to have. I know you know the subject matter as good as anyone alive. The story is of your friend and mine, Frankie Laine. If this interests you, let me know, and I'll fill you in with all the reasons for my request. Because of Frank's situation, I'm having to change my approach. If you're interested, I'll make it all clear.*
>
> *Regards,*
>
> *Jimmy*

That evening, after work, I telephoned and Jimmy shocked me by asking me if I would be interested in doing some writing for the documentary and also hosting the entire production. I couldn't believe it! I was overjoyed! Jimmy wanted me to act as the on-camera historian who segued back and forth between the celebrity interviews. He also asked me to write a script based upon the idea he was sending me. I was excited beyond my wildest imagination. I couldn't wait to telephone Marlene and tell her the news. She was so proud of me after hearing of my good fortune. We went to the restaurant where we first met and celebrated. Life is, indeed, great!

That fall and winter I worked tirelessly writing a forty-thousand-word script for the documentary.

Since I was going to have a major involvement in the Frankie Laine documentary, I took it upon myself to make sure certain key people Frankie had worked with over the years were located and interviewed. I recommended several of these people to Jimmy. My recommendations included Jimmy Boyd, Jerome Courtland, Connie Haines, Lucy Marlow, Terry Moore, and Constance Towers. As always, Jimmy was grateful for the assistance.

I also deemed it important that Jimmy interview famed singer Jo Stafford for the documentary. She played a major role in Frankie's career. During the early 1950s, the two recorded many duets together and even recorded an album.

I wrote Miss Stafford a letter asking permission to interview her for the documentary. Shortly thereafter, I was at the same time both happy and dejected when I arrived home from work one evening and discovered Jo Stafford had left a recorded message for me on my telephone voice mail system. Basically, she kindly asked to "beg off" this project, because she no longer performs on television. Although admitting she loves Frankie, she kindly declined our invitation to be interviewed. I really intended for her to be a part of the documentary, but certainly respected her wishes. At any rate, I was totally blown away by receiving this message from such a superstar. *Damn! I wish I'd have been home! How wonderful it would have been to talk with Jo Stafford.*

I also wrote to Tony Bennett, Mel Brooks, Doris Day, and Clint Eastwood, but for some unknown reason I never received a reply from any of them.

I contacted SAG, the Screen Actors Guild, in search of Jimmy Boyd, the child singer Frankie recorded with. After several weeks of searching, they were unable to track down Boyd. After an Internet search, I went as far as sending an e-mail to his former wife. She was helpful, but nothing panned out.

I also contacted a lady by e-mail who, I'd discovered, was an acquaintance of Jack Haley, Jr. Seemingly, Boyd and Haley were good friends. She returned an e-mail informing me she had asked Haley if he knew Jimmy Boyd's whereabouts, on my behalf. He informed her he'd seen Jimmy recently, but unfortunately, had no contact information. Sadly, about a week later, Haley died suddenly. I was hoping he would be a future guide in helping us track down Jimmy.

I soon received what I thought was a good lead regarding an e-mail address for Jimmy Boyd. I wrote to this address, asking if this was the great child singer Jimmy Boyd. I received a quick reply on the same day that simply stated, *YES*. I was thrilled! *Great! I found him at last!*

I replied with a long note asking if he would kindly allow us to interview him for the Frankie Laine documentary since he had played an important role in Frankie's career. In short order I received a reply that basically informed me, to my utter shock, that he would be glad to do the interview if I brought along a . . . *whore to suck my* [his] *big dick.* I guess this "charming" person wasn't the great Jimmy Boyd, after all. I was duped. I became very angry. I wrote back stating our sincerity in attempting to locate the wonderful singing star Jimmy Boyd to interview for the Frankie Laine documentary. I added how sad it was for us to receive such garbage as a reply for our efforts. I sent the e-mail, but never received a reply. I couldn't have cared less. The real Jimmy Boyd remained elusive.

Through SAG, I received information on three people who were in Frankie Laine's movies for Columbia Pictures—Jerome Courtland, Arthur Franz, and Lucy Marlow. In my opinion, it was important to have these people in Frankie's documentary. I deemed it especially important to include Jerome Courtland and Lucy Marlow. Both appeared in more than one film with Frankie.

On a whim, I sent an e-mail to famed documentary producer Ken Burns (who I later had the privilege of meeting in person) to find out if any organization existed that was dedicated to assisting documentary producers in locating celebrities. He sent a prompt reply:

> *Sir,*
>
> *Thanks for your note . . . . I'm sorry to say that there is no one clearing house of information that we use. In fact, we like the detective aspect of documentary filmmaking— having to track down those elusive family members and*

> *long gone stars, etc. That's the fun. SAG is a good source,*
> *but shoe leather, virtual as well as literal, is what works*
> *best for us. Good Luck.*
>
> *Ken Burns*

Procedure dictates that SAG must first call their members, and they, in turn, are given the telephone number of those who wish to contact them. Then the celebrities make contact, if they so choose. That was the way it was with Jimmy Boyd. Strangely, SAG had numbers of several Jimmy Boyds and called them all, giving them my telephone number. A couple of Jimmy Boyds called SAG back relating they weren't the singing Jimmy Boyd we were seeking. The others never returned calls to SAG or to me.

Jerome Courtland starred in three of Frankie's movies—*Make Believe Ballroom, When You're Smiling,* and *Sunny Side of the Street.* Frankie shared star billing on the latter two. Arthur Franz starred in the movie *Rainbow 'Round My Shoulder,* which also featured Frankie. Lucy Marlow was featured with Frankie in *Bring Your Smile Along* and shared the star billing spotlight with Frankie on *He Laughed Last.*

For some unknown reason, after being contacted, Arthur Franz never called back. I was beginning to get frustrated, but it was short-lived. One day at work, I received a special telephone call.

"Hello, Craig? This is Jerry Courtland."

"Are you the same Jerome Courtland who starred in three movies with Frankie Laine?" I asked, in a profound daze.

"Yes, about a hundred years ago," he chuckled.

We had a pleasant conversation, and he agreed to be interviewed for the documentary. Courtland asked that I call him "Jerry." From then on,

Jerry and I became telephone pals for a while. We exchanged calls quite a lot.

After giving it much thought, I contacted Jimmy Marino and asked permission to interview Jerome Courtland myself. I was trained in media production, and since Jerry lived in Chicago, I was closer and could save Jimmy's crew the expense of traveling from California to conduct the interview. Jimmy readily agreed to let me handle the task. I also suggested he allow me to interview Frankie's brother, Phil LoVecchio, since he, too, lived in Chicago.

After informing me he'd get back to me, Jimmy held a meeting with Frankie's conductor and arranger, Benny Hollman, and they both agreed to allow me to also interview Phil.

With permission granted from Jimmy, all I needed to do was coordinate the date, places, and times for both interviews. I was excited and so was Marlene. I was happy she wanted to tag along with me.

After several telephone calls to both Jerry and Phil, the Chicago interviews were set for October 7, 2000. Our itinerary was arranged so we'd arrive at Jerry Courtland's home first, then meet with Phil. Marlene and I rented a Super VHS video camera and borrowed lighting equipment. Finally, we were ready for another adventure together!

We arrived at Jerry Courtland's home right on schedule. I knocked on his door. After a brief wait, he opened the door. "Hi, Craig. I'm Jerry Courtland," he said as he extended his hand. "Do you need any help carrying things in?" In turn, I introduced Marlene to Jerry and we all three carried in camera cases, bags, and other equipment for the interview.

Jerry was still slender and extremely tall. He maintained the eyebrows that shaped into a point toward his forehead whenever he smiled or became amused. These resemblances mirrored the shy, awkward young man he portrayed in Frankie's movies. The similarities stopped there. Jerry's hair was now thin on top and his face more filled out and weathered. He wore glasses, and his speaking voice was of a lower register than when he was young. Jerry no longer looked young and innocent. Film had captured his image and held on to his youth. The movies kept him young. Real life had not been so kind.

As I was setting things up at the Courtland residence, we enjoyed a casual conversation. I couldn't believe I was in Jerry's home preparing to interview him! It was like I was in a dream. Jerry's home was beautiful and comfortable-looking. Simple, yet elegant furniture decorated the wooden floors.

"We have pastries here if you're hungry," Jerry offered. "Would you like a cup of coffee?" he added.

Gladly, I accepted a cup of coffee while asking Jerry where I could plug in my lights. After taking a few sips, I set down my half-finished cup of coffee and continued to work setting up the equipment. When I had things ready to go, I searched for my coffee. It had seemingly vanished.

"I can't find my coffee," I reported to Jerry.

"Oh, I drank it. I was afraid it would get cold," he readily admitted.

I was delighted. *Just think, Jerome Courtland finished drinking my cup of coffee!*

I simply couldn't fathom I was in the presence of the tall, skinny kid who was so charming in three of Frankie Laine's movies. I watched these movies over and over for almost fifteen years and never dreamt someday I would meet Jerome Courtland face to face, let alone be in his beautiful home sharing a cup of coffee.

Many people don't realize that Jerome Courtland sang the title theme song to the Walt Disney classic movie *Old Yeller*. In addition to working with many great stars on film, Jerry later went on to work in television. Adding to his numerous television guest roles, he also starred in two different series, *The Saga of Andy Burnett* and *Tales of the Vikings*. Later, he became a movie producer and a television director.

Prior to our trip to visit Jerry and Phil, I asked Jimmy Marino if he would speak to Frankie to obtain permission for me to call him on the day I interviewed Jerome Courtland. I formulated the idea to call Frankie from Jerry's house at a specified time, using my calling card, to allow Jerry to speak with Frankie. This would be sort of a telephone reunion between two old movie pals. It would be my gift to both stars.

Jimmy promptly sent me a return e-mail stating Frankie would be delighted to receive my call at ten o'clock California time on the day I visited Jerome Courtland. It was noon in Chicago when I informed Jerry I had a surprise for him. "I've made it possible, in advance, to telephone Frankie Laine at his home so you two could chat," I beamed. "This will be on my dime," I added. Jerry was pleased.

I asked permission to use his telephone and dialed Frankie's number. When Frankie answered, I informed him he was about to speak with Jerry Courtland, as my treat. Then, I handed the phone to Jerry. As these two old friends chitchatted, I sat there watching, almost in tears. It was unbelievable. I made it possible to reunite these two wonderful stars after all these years. I'll always remember that moment.

Prior to the interview, as we were talking, I was thrilled when Jerry reminisced about working with Humphrey Bogart in the 1949 Columbia movie *Tokyo Joe*. "He was just an older guy, and I didn't think too much about it," he said.

My interview with Jerry was very informative. Jerry was very patient with me while I posed the questions needed for the documentary. Of course, only a small portion of the interview would make the final cut, but I asked them all, nonetheless.

When I inquired what it was like working with Frankie Laine in the movies, Jerry answered:

> *"I had started as just an actor—a non-singing actor— and when I had the opportunity work with Frankie . . . it really was exciting to me . . . . I'd always been a huge fan."*

It was interesting to discover Jerry's feelings upon actually getting the chance to sing with Frankie in two of the three movies:

> *"To be able to watch him on stage is one thing, but when you can work in a film with him and see really how he rehearsed, how he did everything—*
>
> *"The story outline, as you know having seen those films, . . . this big star, Frankie Laine, who helps this kid . . . become a singer. Well, in reality it gave me the same opportunity. So there's a parallel there that's pretty interesting."*

I was thrilled with Jerry's reply to my question regarding an interesting story he might recall involving Frankie. Jerry's answer was a classic portrayal of Frankie Laine's generous nature. This was the clip Jimmy ultimately used a portion of in the finished documentary:

"The most memorable story was not on the set, it was when we first started rehearsing the musical numbers together. Frankie can sing a little higher than I can. And rather than forcing me—when they were setting the keys— as you know, every singer has a key in which the range of the music falls more comfortably for certain singers in certain keys. And Frankie being the big musical star, could have said 'no . . . the kid's gonna do it in my key.' But he didn't. He said to the musical director, . . . 'I'll do it in Jerry's key.' Which really impressed me. As I say, I remember it to this day. He did it in my key to accommodate me—in both films that I sang with him in."

Jerry went on to say that he learned a lot from Frankie simply by observing him. He actually made it a point to attend Frankie's musical rehearsals, learning much from Frankie.

"Because he was so good—he knew so much—he was such a great musician, . . . he gave me the opportunity to study him."

Jerry's favorite movie of the three was *Sunny Side of the Street*. Jerry disclosed his reasons:

"We had more scenes together. Instead of singing one number as I did in 'Make Believe Ballroom,' two

numbers in 'When You're Smiling,' this one I got to do three numbers. I got to sing with Frankie again—we did a duet—that's why it was my favorite."

I wanted to know if Jerry was recognized by fans after appearing in Frankie's films. He chuckled and acknowledged he was. He went on to say that sometimes fans would ask him if he actually sang in the movies:

"One of the questions was, did I sing for myself or was my voice being dubbed? . . . [B]ecause at that time, as you know, a lot of the actors—that was back in the days of musicals—and a lot of big stars who did not sing were still doing musicals. Rita Hayworth, for example. Her voice was dubbed. A lot of major stars. And so it wasn't at all uncommon. So a lot of people thought my voice was being dubbed."

Later, after the interview, I asked Jerry if he did, indeed, sing his own songs in those movies, and he adamantly proclaimed he sang in all three, and his voice was never dubbed.

During his interview, Jerry described the process of singing in the movies:

"When we sing on film—when we sing in a scene—the music is always prerecorded. Then you sing to a playback. It's because when we shoot a scene, we never shoot it just as a master. We shoot, say, a wide shot of it, then a little tighter, and a little tighter, and so forth. But if you were singing to an actual orchestra onstage at that time, and you went from the master at one tempo with the orchestra, and I don't

care how good the orchestra is, if they play it a second time there's no way it's gonna be the exact same tempo. So now when they move in for a close-up, or whatever coverage they would want, you would have a different tempo. And then if they move to a different close-up, you'd still have a different tempo. So when they try to intercut them, they're all edited—as we know, . . . it just wouldn't work."

Jerry told me he always enjoyed Frankie's voice. He particularly liked Frankie's vocal delivery. He also studied how Frankie worked an audience.

"To have the opportunity to study Frankie time and time and time again and watch him work that audience and see what he did to affect the audience—to really reach them and have them enjoy him—it was a cram course in presentation."

I wanted Jerry's opinion on Frankie as an actor, and Jerry affirmed that Frankie was very good at acting. Jerry spoke about, as a young man, working with some actors who were difficult. He laughed as he recalled:

"In one case I did a film with Rosalind Russell . . . called 'A Woman of Distinction,' with Rosalind Russell and Ray Milland. In that . . . they had me playing this kind of shy, awkward kid next door. And they gave me a lot of laugh lines; they gave me the jokes. And Rosalind Russell wasn't too pleased with that. So, Miss Russell had the script rewritten so that I did the feed line and she did the jokes. But Frankie would never have done anything like that."

234

At the end of my interview, I asked Jerry to look into the camera and say something directly to Frankie. I asked him to begin by stating his name as "Jerome Courtland," because this was his famous professional name:

"Hi, Frankie, this is Jerome Courtland, better known to you as Jerry Courtland. . . . I sure wish you were here. I wish you were here so you could help me remember some of these things. Craig is asking me some very good questions, and it was a long time ago. And anyway, I just would enjoy seeing you and reminiscing and thinking about old times and the fun working with you on the set. If you come through Chicago, gotta give me a buzz. Craig has my number, and it would really be great to see you. Anyway, from a couple of thousand miles away I gotta say 'hi,' and I think about you a lot. Take good care."

All during the interview, Marlene used our home video camera to shoot footage of Jerry and me. This was sort of a "behind-the-scenes" compilation for my collection. We both loved our visit with Jerry. I felt a special bond with this nice man. After saying good-bye to Jerry, and giving him a hug, Marlene and I headed out to meet with Phil LoVecchio.

Phil greeted us and, like before at Jerry's, we chatted while I set up my equipment. Phil is an extremely interesting man in his own right. It was nice to talk with him. When the camera was rolling, however, I was rather taken aback by Phil's answer to my first question. I asked him what it was like growing up with Frankie:

"Well, I really don't remember him when I was a kid. Because he was gone—on the road—tryin' to make it in

show business. So, I don't remember him, until, of course,
he became famous."

I wanted to know what the rest of their siblings thought of Frankie's success:

"I think everybody was as thrilled as I was. You tend
to bask in the reflective glory. I mean it was a kick. I was
thrilled when I knew this was my brother, Frankie Laine.
They were the same. Everybody was just happy as they
could be."

Phil went on to say he first realized Frankie was famous when he began to hear Frankie's records, such as Frankie's first big hit, "That's My Desire," being played on the radio. It was informative to discover how Phil was treated at the time Frankie first became famous:

"The kids in the neighborhood, they thought it was
pretty neat that I had a famous brother; it was 'kicky.'"

After Frankie became famous, Phil informed me Frankie had their father retire. Frankie relocated their mother and father, along with Phil, to a house he bought them in Burbank, California. One of the best quotes from Phil, which ultimately made it into Jimmy's Frankie Laine birthday video, regarded Frankie's newfound fame:

"It was amazing the people that wanted to get to see
him backstage—all the kids—that was really interesting.
There were hundreds, if not thousands, of kids after every
show."

I wanted to know what Phil's favorite Frankie Laine recorded song was. Phil agreed there were many but chose "Granada," recorded by Frankie in 1953, as his favorite. Phil went on to relate how devastated Frankie was when his friend, pianist, accompanist, and song-writing partner Carl Fischer died in 1954:

> *"They were like brothers because they started together.*
>
> *But, he* [Frankie] *went on—what else is there to do?"*

Phil revealed that their mother especially enjoyed Frankie's fame. According to Phil, she had his pictures everywhere in the house. At any given moment, she could tell anybody where Frankie was playing an engagement. She knew everything there was to know about her son, Frankie Laine. Phil recounted that his best gift from Frankie was when Frankie flew his entire family to Las Vegas to celebrate their parents' fiftieth wedding anniversary.

Just as I did with Jerry, I asked Phil to say something to Frankie while looking directly into the camera:

> *"Brother Frank, stay well. Keep on doin' whatever*
> *it is you're doin'. Keep on singin'. Because you ARE a*
> *singer, and this IS your song."*

Back home a few days after I sent Jerry a copy of his video interview, we talked on the telephone one evening. Jerry fascinated me with a behind-the-scenes mental picture during the course of the filming of one of his movies.

In the 1950 Columbia movie *A Woman of Distinction,* during the car scene close-up where Jerry was with Rosalind Russell, Jerry explained that she had on a gown with a flowing cape. When shooting the close-ups in the car—a convertible—the car was actually in a studio, and the director used rear screen projection footage depicting the outer movement. Thus, the car seemed to be in motion. To reinforce this illusion, a fan was utilized to simulate the wind.

During the camera shoot, Rosalind Russell's cape was not flowing backwards, which would indicate the car was moving forward. Jerry, in an attempt to be helpful, suggested to the director that they place a piece of wire underneath and connect it to the end of the cape so it would give the impression that the cape was trailing behind in the wind.

According to Jerry, the director became somewhat belligerent because Jerry, a mere kid, attempted to give him, the experienced director, advice. In the end, however, Jerry's idea was used. Nevertheless, in the scene showing the close-up inside the moving car, it's obvious the cape was held up by a wire.

It was wonderful getting to know both Jerry and Phil. Jimmy Marino loved my taped interview footage. Things were great! The documentary was on a roll. After reviewing my video of the interviews, I received a touching e-mail from Jimmy:

> *Craig,*
>
> *I just got your tape, and I put it right on, and I sure am glad I met you!!!! You did a great job, and you should feel very proud of what you did and are doing for Frankie and those of us who love him. I can't thank you enough for all your help. If you were here I would HUG you, so consider yourself HUGGED!!*
>
> *Fellow Documentarian,*
>
> *Jimmy*

During the Christmas season of 2001, Marlene and I received a special gift from Jerry Courtland and his wife. They sent us a replica of a vintage

1930s cocktail shaker designed to look like a penguin. This chrome treasure is displayed on a special wall shelf in our living room.

* * *

I received another pleasantly shocking telephone call at work one day. The voice on the other end of the line was unforgettable.

"Hello, Craig. This is Lucy Marlow."

Lucy and I talked for several minutes. She definitely wanted to be a part of Frankie's documentary, and gave me all her contact information, which I later passed along to Jimmy. It was delightful talking to this great lady. She is very nice and extremely interesting. She related stories about Frankie during the filming of *Bring Your Smile Along* and *He Laughed Last.* "Frankie took a bunch of the cast and crew from one of the films to his parents' home," Lucy explained. "Frankie's father gave us a tour of his basement, and they had sausages and meats hanging from the ceiling. It was incredible," she added.

Lucy related how Frankie gave her career a boost. "Frankie insisted I receive top billing along with him on *He Laughed Last,*" she proclaimed. She also serenaded me over the phone. *Lucy Marlow singing to me?! Wow!*

I had to give Marlene the latest news regarding the mesmerizing telephone call I'd just received, so I telephoned her at work. She thought it was wonderful that Lucy got in touch with me.

During my reign within the production of the documentary, I also mentioned to Jimmy Marino that we should attempt to locate singer Connie Haines and actresses Terry Moore and Constance Towers to be interviewed. He agreed and we both began searching for them.

Meanwhile, Frankie's first CD box set, incorporating his entire Mercury Records catalog, was released. Tony Cooper worked diligently on this masterpiece. In the October FLSOA newsletter, a quote of mine was printed regarding the production:

> *Tony and everyone associated with the project did a*
> *fantastic job.*

In the December 2000 issue of the FLSOA newsletter, I became the very first Frankie Laine fan to be featured in "Fan Profile," a new segment in the newsletter. I wrote a short feature entitled "Cronbaugh/Laine Chronicle."

One of my old letter-writing buddies, John Welsh from Canada, mentioned my name in a piece that he wrote, which was published in the March 2001 issue of the FLSOA newsletter. John and I had corresponded during the 1980s, both seeking certain Frankie Laine songs for our respective collections. We were able to assist each other with elusive Laine material.

Finally finishing my documentary script, I sent copies to both Jimmy and Frankie. Jimmy was impressed after reading it. He deemed it too long, but I assured him I could cut it down. Frankie was impressed with my research skills. He suggested that I transform my script into a manuscript for a book.

During March 2001, in my attempt to make certain Connie Haines, Lucy Marlow, and Terry Moore were lined up for interviews with Jimmy for the documentary, I had pleasant telephone conversations with each.

While talking with Connie Haines, I couldn't help recalling each taped television episode I'd seen of *The Frankie Laine Show*. The show originally aired in 1954 and 1955. Connie was featured with Frankie on this syndicated show. Prior to our phone conversation, Connie had sent me an autographed copy of her new book, *Snootie Little Cutie*. She also sent me an audiocassette of one of her albums.

Connie sang with Tommy Dorsey's band in the 1940s, when Frank Sinatra and Buddy Rich were also members. Among my musical collections, I have old film footage on video of her from that era, as well. While talking with Connie, I couldn't help thinking of watching her perform on the video with Rich and Sinatra. It's a miracle I stayed focused. I loved every minute!

I watched Lucy Marlow perform in *Bring Your Smile Along* and *He Laughed Last* over and over for many years. The same feelings that I had whenever conversing with Jerry Courtland came over me when I talked to her over the phone.

During this, our second telephone conversation, Lucy and I discussed both Frankie and the documentary. The work in progress was interesting to her. She was thrilled to be a part of it. She was grateful that I contacted her so Jimmy could set up an interview. Lucy spoke about her two Frankie Laine films. She was disappointed that those movies were not available for purchase on video.

"Enjoy your interview with Jimmy," I said to her at the end of our conversation.

"Thank you, Craig," Lucy replied.

"Say nice things about me to Jimmy, okay?" I quipped. "I think I already have," she rejoined.

After watching Terry Moore in *Sunny Side of the Street,* not to mention Mom's favorite movie, *Come Back, Little Sheba,* it was mind-boggling to realize I was actually speaking to her! I wished Mom was still alive to share in my excitement. During a previous telephone conversation with Terry, just after my interview with Jerry Courtland, she spoke quite a bit about her late husband, Howard Hughes (according to Terry, they never divorced). She acknowledged that Frankie Laine was Hughes' favorite singer. However, during this particular call, she was interested in knowing all about what was currently going on in Frankie's life. I had previously sent her a video copy of the movie *Sunny Side of the Street,* and to my amazement, she told me this was the first time she had ever watched it. "I was thrilled to see it; I was delighted! Thank you!" Terry exclaimed.

Terry and I spoke about Frankie's current throat problems. She wanted very much to know how he was doing.

"What do you think the secret to his youth is?" Terry asked me.

"His music and his audiences and his fans. I think he gets so much pleasure out of that. . . . [T]hat keeps him young at heart," I replied.

I also had sent Terry copies of some of the lobby cards for *Sunny Side of the Street.*

"Did you get the posters?" I asked her.

"Oh, yes! I can't thank you enough!" she joyously exclaimed.

I was elated when she asked me for my phone number and address so she could keep in touch with me. We talked a little about Jerry Courtland, who starred with her in *Sunny Side of the Street.* She knew I was in touch with Jerry because of my work on the documentary. Terry also gave me information on how to reach a couple of stars we were interested in contacting for Frankie's documentary. Then it was time to sign off. "Good luck, sweetheart, that's all I can do for now," she said. I spoke my good-bye to her and she followed with, "Okay, honey, good-bye." *Wow! Terry Moore called me both "sweetheart" AND "honey"!*

I enjoyed chatting with each of these three ladies, all giant stars in their own right. I almost pinched myself from time to time during each conversation.

* * *

My own lady was becoming more and more special to me. I decided I wanted to spend the rest of my life with Marlene. She and I proved to ourselves that we were in love and wanted to be together always. This spring was destined to be busy, happy, and memorable. From the beginning of our relationship, our favorite Frankie Laine love song became "Making Memories," recorded by Frankie in 1967 for ABC Records.

Marlene's son Matt and daughter-in-law Chris were expecting their first child in April. Marlene was ecstatic! She wanted a little grandbaby to love. That's one of the things I adore about Marlene—she is full of love to give and share.

Latisha and her fiancé, Jermey, were planning a wedding in April, as well. I was very happy because I knew how much he meant to my daughter.

As their wedding date drew nearer, Marlene and I were concerned that the grandbaby might arrive on the same date Tish and Jermey were going to be married. This apprehension escalated since Tish lived, and would be married, close to one hundred miles from Des Moines. Marlene was prepared to remain "on call" in case she had to leave the wedding and drive back to Des Moines for the birth of the grandbaby.

Everything worked out and on April 21, 2001, Latisha and Jermey were married. I cried continuously throughout the ceremony from the moment I first saw Tish in her wedding gown, proudly walking her down the aisle, and all during the wedding and afterwards in the receiving line. It was an extremely emotional day for me. My beautiful daughter, my little girl, was getting married.

My old band, with Don Daugherty and Glenn Goodwin, played at the reception following the wedding. Dan Boddicker, who also attended the wedding, brought along his keyboards and played with the band. Mitch Smith, Dan's friend and ours from Dan's own band, also came along to sit in and play saxophone. All my friends together! It was a fantastic evening. The grandbaby waited for us.

One week later, to the day, after Latisha was married, Chris was admitted to the hospital to deliver the baby we all were waiting for. Matt, Marlene, and I were on hand in and out of Chris's room, anxiously awaiting the arrival.

During a break from the anticipation, I found a moment to be alone with Matt.

"I have a very important question to ask you," I began.

"Okay," Matt replied, somewhat dubious.

"Since you're the most important person in your mom's life, not to mention the most important man, I need to ask you this," I said in a matter-of-fact way.

Matt nodded his understanding. "Sure," he replied.

"May I have permission to marry your mom?" I asked breathlessly.

"Yes," Matt answered immediately. "We all knew you two would get together eventually," he added with a smile.

"Thanks, Matt. That means a lot," I said. "I knew I couldn't marry her without first asking your permission."

I informed him that I was going to propose the very next day.

Soon after asking Matt's permission to marry his mom, Payton was born. This beautiful little baby girl arrived, transforming Matt and Chris into parents and Marlene into a grandma. Best of all, I was a grandpa! And, after tomorrow's proposal, I would eventually officially become a member of the family!

I had something special planned for my proposal. The restaurant where Marlene and I first met had been sold to new owners and was closed for renovation. I noticed an article in the newspaper regarding the project and the new owner. I contacted the writer of the article and obtained the owner's telephone number. I got in touch with this man and explained my plan. I asked if he would assist me by opening up the restaurant long enough for me to decorate the booth where my fiancée and I first met, so I could propose to her. Obviously a romantic at heart, he agreed to go along with my scheme.

We set up a time on the planned day. The owner let me in, and I was free to decorate the very booth Marlene and I first sat at one year earlier. I brought in a dozen roses, balloons, wine, anniversary decorations, and candles. Even though the place was actually boarded up and debris from the renovation was strewn about, our booth was like an oasis, charmed with decorations and hopeful expectations.

I picked Marlene up in the afternoon on the day after Payton was born. It was also the first anniversary of the day we met. She had no idea what I had planned.

"Where are you taking me?" Marlene asked in a skeptical tone.

"I thought we'd ride around for awhile and maybe get out and walk around the area where we first met," I answered ever so craftily.

We parked and started walking.

"Let's walk to the front of the place where we met," I suggested.

When we arrived there, I ushered Marlene inside the big door leading to an entranceway, also used for access to upstairs apartments. Off to the far side was the boarded-up door to "our" restaurant. Casually, I walked over to the plywood-covered door.

"Hey, it's open," I informed Marlene.

"Don't go in there because it's shut down," she replied, obviously dubious.

"I just want to open the door a crack and look in," I countered. I opened the door and took Marlene's hand and felt her pull away.

"Don't go in there," she pleaded.

"I only want to take a look," I said in a dramatic way. It was all I could do to pull Marlene through the door of the renovation debris-laden restaurant.

Once inside, Marlene spotted the decorated booth. I led her to our special area. She couldn't speak. I poured us some wine and went over to her. I got down on one knee and handed her a diamond ring and proposed. I had tears in my eyes the whole time, and Marlene was crying. Then she said the three magic words: "Yes, yes, yes." I had a radio there, and we danced and drank our wine. It was a time forever etched in our memories.

* * *

I thought it was high time Frankie Laine was officially recognized for his achievements in music. In May, I sent a long submission letter to the National Academy of Recording Arts and Sciences, Incorporated. My intent was to recommend Frankie to receive the Recording Academy's Lifetime Achievement Award. On July 16, 2001, I received this letter:

> *Dear Mr. Cronbaugh:*
>
> *This letter is to confirm that we have received your submission of Frankie Laine for the Recording Academy's Lifetime Achievement Award. Mr. Laine will be on the official list of recommendations to be reviewed and voted on by our Trustees in May of 2002.*
>
> *While the Trustees vote on these recommendations in May, the Academy does not usually announce the winners until sometime in late November. Shortly before the public release of this information, we contact each award winner. We do not contact individuals to let them know that their names have been submitted.*

To my utter dismay, Frankie never received the award. In my opinion, nobody deserved it more, but he wasn't selected to receive it. I never understood why. Seemingly, every other past and present musical star has received the honor except Frankie Laine. I found this very sad. Worst of all, it was painfully obvious that there was nothing I could do to remedy the situation.

My personal life was happy, however. Marlene and I were married on October 20, 2001. We were married on the second-floor rotunda in the Iowa State Capitol. In addition to our family and friends, three Iowa state representatives were present for the ceremony. After we were married, we held a reception complete with two bands. My old band, with Don Daugherty and Glenn Goodwin, performed, as did Dan Boddicker's band. I considered myself to be a blessed and happy man.

A couple of days before we spoke our vows, we received a large box from Frankie and Marcia Laine. To our joyful surprise, the box contained a bottle of champagne from the LoVecchio orchards to commemorate our marriage. The champagne, named *Symphony Laine,* was a very special gift. Along with the champagne, Frankie included an autographed copy of his new CD, *Teach Me to Pray*—a new release of inspirational songs he recorded and released years before—and a card. On the CD cover Frankie wrote that he wished us as much happiness in our married life as he and Marcia enjoyed.

That evening, I telephoned Frankie and thanked him for their thoughtful gift box. "You're welcome. Enjoy," he answered, his voice still raspy. He informed me he was going to go into the studio the very next day to attempt to record a song. "I doubt if I'll be successful," he told me. It was sad to hear the great Frankie Laine say this.

Then Marlene chatted with Frankie on the telephone. "You take care of him; he's a good guy," Frankie told her at the end of their conversation. These were the same words he spoke to her as he hugged her good-bye during our last visit to the Laine home in July 2000.

The recording session Frankie spoke to me about resulted in his rendition of "My Buddy/Taps," added to a lineup of patriotic and uplifting-type songs he recorded years ago. The CD was entitled *Together Again, My Buddy*. Although somewhat subdued, Frankie's voice is beautiful on the new song.

Frankie had been experiencing trouble with his voice since the beginning of 2000. What began as a node on the front of his left vocal cord went on to include a squamous cell tumor on the backside. Both the node and tumor were subsequently removed. Frankie also underwent radiation therapy. During the time he was suffering with throat ailments, he wasn't able to perform and could hardly speak for a couple of years.

* * *

As the documentary project moved onward, Jimmy was unfortunately becoming disenchanted with tracking down elusive celebrities to be interviewed, and he was experiencing difficulty selling the idea of Frankie's documentary to television stations.

My glory ride came abruptly to an end when Jimmy informed me that he decided that in order to make Frankie's documentary "sellable," he was forced to turn the project over to a seasoned documentary staff. Therefore, in an instant, the Frankie Laine documentary acquired a new writer. Jimmy turned over all his interview footage, Frankie's autobiography, and my script to this new production team. He assured me my script was being utilized for certain facts I'd researched, and I would receive an on-screen research credit at the end of the documentary.

I was no longer a major player in the production of the documentary, and I was crushed and angry. I vented all my frustrations to Jimmy and

Mary-Jo. Thankfully, those wonderful people were able to overlook my temporary insanity. I felt like someone who had won the lottery only to be told they must give all the money back several months later. I gave my heart and soul to the documentary out of my love for Frankie. I was proud I played such an important role in helping Jimmy make this production a success. I wondered if any of my original on-camera interview would even make the final cut. To say I was despondent would be an understatement.

Gradually, as the weeks went by, I began to feel better. I realized I played a major role in the documentary,-after all, because of all the work I'd put into it. My interviews, phone calls, and months of writing the script testified to that. Jimmy was attempting to make the documentary a success. He utilized the only method available to him. With my new state of mind, I felt better. I recognized my former role in the production simply wasn't meant to be. I would not perform the on-camera commentary, nor be the writer. Slowly, I accepted this. Famed singer Lou Rawls eventually became the on-camera host.

When the documentary was completed, I received a screen credit for my research. And, most importantly, I was the only American Frankie Laine fan to be featured on-camera in Frankie's historic documentary.

During my on-screen portion of the documentary, I said:

> *"When Frankie sings, he doesn't just read the lyrics off a sheet of music. He actually makes you believe, just as a storyteller makes you believe in a story—a narrator; Frankie was able to put across in his music what he was singing about. And that's something very rare in a singer, especially these days."*

After all was said and done, I was, indeed, a part of Frankie's history. I suddenly felt happy, fulfilled, and proud. Jimmy Marino became my champion. Because of him, I remained a part of the production. I achieved exactly what I endeavored when I first contacted Mary-Jo years earlier and asked her who was producing the Frankie Laine documentary. Another quest was realized. It was hard won, but totally worth all the effort and strife.

Ringo Starr was a featured celebrity in the documentary. It was because of Ringo that I first became interested in playing the drums. I idolized the Beatles. Now, I was a part of the same production Ringo was involved in. As far as I was concerned, this was an incredible way to look at the big picture. The documentary, entitled *Frankie Laine: An American Dreamer,* was released in November 2003. The featured celebrities included Pat Boone, Dick Clark, Maria Cole, Jerome Courtland, Shecky Greene, Connie Haines, Herb Jeffries, Jack Jones, Howard Keel, Michel Legrand, Mundell Lowe, A.C. Lyles, Lucy Marlow, Peter Marshall, Mitch Miller, Terry Moore, Sammy Nestico, Patti Page, Kay Starr, Ringo Starr, Constance Towers, and John Williams.

I don't keep in touch with Jerry Courtland too much these days. I send him birthday and Christmas cards, and he will send an occasional letter. Like most stars that are retired, Jerry wishes to remain somewhat aloof, and I respect that. Lucy Marlow and I keep in touch by telephone a couple of times a year. I really enjoy chatting with this special lady.

Latisha gave birth to a son, Keon, on February 17, 2003. Now, Marlene and I are blessed with both a granddaughter and a grandson!

My most recent Frankie Laine friend is Mark Gallagher from Virginia. Mark and I became friends after he diligently assembled a fantastic Frankie Laine Internet site. We sometimes send items to each other in order to build up our respective Frankie Laine collections. Mark is a true friend because I trust him enough to inform him, through e-mail, what's on my mind. I especially bend his ear when I'm disenchanted with anything within the Frankie Laine domain. I treasure my friendship with Mark.

On the photograph page of Mark's site the picture of Frankie Laine and me, taken when I visited Frankie's home in 1999, is featured.

Marlene and I booked a flight to San Diego to attend the tribute to celebrate Frankie's ninetieth birthday on March 30, 2003, in the Grand Ballroom of the U.S. Grant Hotel.

The day we arrived, I telephoned Frankie, hoping to set up an interview with him for an idea I had for this book. He was happy to oblige, and we set up a time to meet the next day.

I telephoned Frankie the following day. Unfortunately, he was ill and we couldn't get together. Even though he wasn't feeling well, he offered to answer a few of my questions. I refused. Never would I impose upon Frankie when he was sick. I told Frankie I'd talk to him at the party the next day. He agreed to this. I was humbled that Frankie was willing to accommodate me even though he was not feeling well.

I never had the opportunity to speak with Frankie during his party either. The crowd was too big, the commotion too overwhelming, and Frankie was still not feeling well and left the party early. I only saw Frankie from the stage where he spoke briefly, giving all in attendance an update on his throat condition. I was very sad I didn't get to visit my old friend face to face.

Marlene and I had the pleasure of meeting famed singers Patti Page and Herb Jeffries, who both attended Frankie's party. Jeffries began as a movie actor portraying the "Bronze Buckaroo" in movies during the late 1930s. These movies were primarily Westerns featuring an all-black cast. He also sang with Duke Ellington's orchestra.

It was enjoyable to give my best to old friends such as Mary-Jo Coombs, Tony Cooper, Marcia Laine, and Jimmy Marino. It was especially nice to see Norman Foster and Stephen Fratallone. I enjoyed introducing all my friends to Marlene.

Marlene and I left the festivities early and headed back to our hotel a few blocks away. We invited Norman and Stephen to our hotel to join us for drinks. When they arrived, we sat in the lounge and enjoyed a few beers. We all had a merry time. When we parted ways, I was melancholy.

"I treasure my Frankie Laine friends," I admitted to Marlene.

"I know, honey," she replied. "I wish they lived closer so you could see them more often."

* * *

Through it all, I enjoy reflecting on my life since Frankie became a part of it. I often recall the first time we met in November 1985. There was a distinct crispness in the Cedar Rapids air. The feelings I took pleasure in during the time just before setting out on my journey were stimulated by the smell of the late autumn air, the enchanting pleasure I derived from reading the Sherlock Holmes stories at night after arriving home from playing music, and the enjoyment of listening to the many Frankie Laine songs Helen Snow sent me.

All of these pleasant sensations were a prelude to my long trip to first meet the man I admired so much. Because my introductory meeting with Frankie was so extraordinary, it is impossible not to also relive certain sensations surrounding that same period in time in much the same way a certain smell might recall a special childhood moment.

I've enjoyed many profoundly happy moments pursuing my Frankie Laine avocation. For years I truly felt I was "in the loop" with Frankie's career. Each time Frankie spoke with me, and every time he displayed kindness, my spirit was renewed. Frankie Laine has more than stimulated me with his musical singing style. He has inspired me to know that I can accomplish wonderful things. All of us can do so much good in our lives if only we believe strongly enough and work diligently toward a purpose. Like most everyone, my life has been interesting, but tinged with sadness. During my lowest hours, I've always counted my blessings. I've tried to look at the brighter side of things.

Achieving my initial quest to meet Frankie Laine is very important to me. In the back of my mind, I believe I can maintain my happiness and accomplish my goals, because I attained my special quest.

I reached out to someone I admire. I believe that a special man received my reach, a living legend who brought me into his world a tiny bit, allowing me to touch his magic. I was transported into a world that I would never have known had it not been for Frankie and his willingness to be my friend. I will always treasure Frankie Laine as my friend. My life is much happier, my soul richer, because he didn't ignore my reaching out.

I took a journey to seek out a star.

From my Iowa home I ventured afar.

The one I sought sang songs from his heart.

My life was made richer by this legend's art.

I sought and I found this singer of fame.

He made me a friend and soon knew my name.

He sings with emotion, inspiring me to feel.

Life has more depth when exhibiting feelings you don't conceal.

He made possible this impossible dream of mine.

Throughout musical history, his star will shine.

I wish to propose an adventure for you:

To yourself, to your hopes, to your dreams be true.

Embark upon a quest; dare to journey afar.

For my life was made happier, reaching for a star.

ABOUT THE AUTHOR

CRAIG CRONBAUGH, Director of the Legislative Information Office with the Legislative Services Agency at the Iowa State Capitol, holds an associate's degree in Communications Media from Kirkwood Community College, Cedar Rapids, Iowa, and a bachelor's degree, *cum laude,* in Communication Broadcast/Broadcast Journalism, with a minor in Political Science, from the University of Northern Iowa, Cedar Falls. He is a former professional musician (drummer) and newspaper editor, writer, and photographer. As a personal friend of famed singer Frankie Laine, and a collector of Laine's recordings and career memorabilia, Craig has written articles; written, produced, directed, and hosted a one-time special radio program; and was featured on television regarding his Frankie Laine avocation. Craig is briefly highlighted and received a research screen credit in the 2003 internationally distributed documentary *Frankie Laine: An American Dreamer.* In addition to having many newspaper articles published, Craig has had a short story featured in an edition of the book *Inner Weather,* published by the University of Northern Iowa, and a poem featured in the book *A Grasp at Eternity,* published by The International Library of Poetry. Craig lives in Des Moines, Iowa, with his wife, Marlene.